Other titles in the UWAP Poetry series (established 2016)

Our Lady of the Fence Post by J. H. Crone

Border Security by Bruce Dawe

Melbourne Journal by Alan Loney

Star Struck by David McCooey

Dark Convicts by Judy Johnson

Flute of Milk by Susan Fealy

A Personal History of Vision by Luke Fischer

Charlie Twirl by Alan Gould

Snake Like Charms by Amanda Joy

Praise for Quinn Eades

Quinn Eades's poetry is an important part of the continuum of the development of language in relation to gender, the body, language and the expression of the self. In *Rallying*, his use of direct language is refreshing. Nothing is too tricky or try-hard-clever so that reading these poems is an amazingly clear experience. Even when he is writing exacting descriptive details there's a clarity and a space for feeling to complement the imagery or the thinking... These poems go against cool, conceptual fashionability. Not many contemporary poets are currently writing embodied poetry and no one is writing quite like Quinn Eades. *Rallying*'s close concern with the female body – especially maternal bodies and relational feeling and thought – is a welcome and distinctive addition to the field of Australian poetry.

Pam Brown

Quinn Eades's writing is poignant and heartbreaking. In a climate of high poetic abstraction, these are refreshing, human poems.

Jessica Wilkinson

Rallying is a generous, full-hearted non-stop call upon experience to tell us what we might need to hear as we make of ourselves what we can, as we change our lives, as we share the smell of two bodies as lovers, as parents with babies, as we inhabit houses that tire of us or celebrate us. From the beggar that wanted to be kissed, to the five-year-old who remarked, 'I just keep moving my legs' as he scaled a mountain, to the sequins that are still stars, these poems know how to sing truly. This is poetry that shows how tough, how sensitive, and full of life free verse still can be.

Kevin Brophy

Rallying

Quinn Eades

Quinn Eades is a researcher, writer, and award-winning poet whose work lies at the nexus of queer, trans, and feminist theories of the body, autobiography, and philosophy. Eades is published nationally and internationally, and is the author of *all the beginnings: a queer autobiography of the body*, published by Tantanoola. He is currently working on his next book, a collection of autobiographical fragments from the body in transition, titled *Trans*positions.

Quinn Eades
Rallying

First published in 2017 by
UWA Publishing
Crawley, Western Australia 6009
www.uwap.uwa.edu.au

UWAP is an imprint of UWA Publishing
a division of The University of Western Australia

This book is copyright. Apart from any fair dealing
for the purpose of private study, research, criticism
or review, as permitted under the *Copyright Act 1968*,
no part may be reproduced by any process without
written permission.
Enquiries should be made to the publisher.

Copyright © Quinn Eades 2017
The moral right of the author has been asserted.

National Library of Australia
Cataloguing-in-Publication entry:
Eades, Quinn, author.
Rallying / Quinn Eades.
ISBN: 9781742589190 (paperback)
Australian poetry.

Designed by Becky Chilcott, Chil3
Typeset in Lyon Text by Lasertype
Printed by Lightning Source

The author has referenced
'Shine on me', Gospel song originally recorded by the
Wiseman Sextette/Quartette in 1923.
"Blackbird." In The Beatles. UK: Apple Records, 1968.

 uwapublishing

For Jem and Soli

Contents

How to disappear in your name 10

Under Them
Shine on me 26
Promise 25
This Mother Thing 26
Milkling 31
The wanting house 33
Creek Walk 35
Ant line 36
Big things break 38
Lay down, lay down 40
Always going home (a domestic cycle) 42
   1. Give (I cannot be separate) 42
   2. A nowhere place (I remember that you are here) 43
   3. The bus home (I am drawn back in) 45
   4. What happens on the other side of the world (I almost split) 47
Small children do not splash or cry out 50

Away With Them
Shiver 54
Sequined 56
Three nights in Kanchanaburi 57
   1. What we want them to see 57
   2. What we carry 59
   3. How we climb 61
More 63
The resort 64
Waiting to be stung 65
Smother 66
Songkran 68
Trawling for tuna 69
Slicing 71
Sail Rock 72
Lanterns on the last night 74
Colder 75

Without Them
In the Alfama **78**
On the metro **80**
Miradouro da Senhora do Monte **81**
Safe Haven **82**
To be kissed **84**
Parque **86**
The Initiate's Well **88**
All I Can Do **90**

Around Them
Separate **92**
Rallying **94**
Echo **96**
Knowings **98**
Salt remembers **99**
Absorption **102**
Ash and breath **104**
Reverberation **107**
Necrosis **109**
Proof **111**
Outline **113**
Gingerly **115**
Coming and Going **116**
Autocorrect is becoming a scourge **118**
Coalesce **124**
Digging **126**

What Comes Next
Glisten **130**
Fruitpicker **131**
Flour **132**
Radiation **133**
The Second Cup **135**
Toe glue (tell) **136**
Swim **137**
Where I Write **140**
Tender Bodies **142**

Acknowledgements **149**

How to disappear in your name

Loving: keeping alive: naming.
Hélène Cixous,
Coming to Writing

                                Call yourself. Give, yourself, names.
                                                          Luce Irigaray,
                                                        To speak is never neutral

PK: PK in the dark in a big big house with SO many stairs and she climbs up them one foot two feet one foot two feet she stops at each one her hand barely reaches the peeling banister her room is at the top of the stairs her room that she shares with her sister with its glass doors that look through to her Mum. With its glass doors that look through that she aches through that she can and can't see through to her Mum.

                                                       body under blankets
                                                     sunk into mattress
                                                     she feels the floor
                                                       against her hip
                                                       the thinness
                                                          of morning

PK in the morning with her sister behind her going down the long long stairs and when she gets to the bottom she is in the lounge-room with her sister behind her and the old red rug is covering the cold cold floorboards and on the old red rug lies a person who is not moving very much at all just an in out in out in out of breath a beer can near an outstretched arm the smell of ash and yeast in the morning she steps over the arm her sister steps over the arm she goes into the kitchen and gets two little wooden bowls her favourite ever bowls and tips in muesli and milk and together, in the ash and yeast and breath, on the old red rug, they eat.

                                                 muesli and milk those
                                                    chewy sultanas
                                                    oats that grind

                                    then rock gravel stone
                                       salted pink milk
                                       a tooth bitten out
                                      a breakfast tooth
                                         an empty gum

PK in the daytime in the corner of the playground where the sandpit is
where she gets a bucket of water and a bucket of sand (a blue bucket of
water and a red bucket of sand) and she adds slowly slowly the water
to the sand and she mixes and mixes and adds and adds until she gets
perfect sand sand to build with sand to touch gravelly and moist sand
that will make houses and humpies and turtle shells and flippers sand
that will sculpture the world.

                                          in the corner
                                         there is shade
                                         the others run
                                       the others chase
                           the others scream squeal the thrill
                                        of being caught
                                          in the corner
                                  the shade keeps the sand
                                    wet graining sculpting
                                           making her
                                         making home

PK in the afternoon after lunch when she didn't like the peas but she
wouldn't get the little cardboard tub of ice-cream with its perfect wooden
paddle that felt grainy on her tongue unless the peas were all gone so
she put them in her mouth and then stored them in her cheeks one by
one then went into the toilets with the long long silver sink and spat the
crushed green balls out and it was the naughtiest thing she'd ever done

and she ate the ice-cream and scraped the paddle on her tongue and then hopped onto her mat and got pat pat patted to sleep by her favourite childcare worker and she slept with a cold belly and a wood feeling on her tongue.

> pale wood paddle
> thin delicate caress
> a tongue that sweeps
> its surface to find
> pine
> breath
> sugared blood
> soursweet
> depth

PK in the dark in the sun it's late they kept saying but she can hear the people walking and see the streak of light under the curtain and birds and everything out there in the sun in the sun in the going down sun.

> light stripped
> of warmth comfort
> coming from heels on concrete
> magpies
> metal striking metal
> all that work
> voices
> talking away time
> waiting for darkness
> for deepening breath
> for caress

BELLA: Bella is the sister-name the one she is called by when needed when loved when wanted for opening jars or reading that story Bella, please, *that* one. Bella is soft she is kind she makes her bed into a nest for her little sister to curl into she stirs porridge in the morning and adds honey and milk. She keeps the sweet thick feel on her tongue for most of the morning (her oaty breath) and then finds her sister at recess and lunch. She sits with her on the long cold silver seats that leave lines on the backs of their thighs. She peels mandarins. She unwraps greaseproof paper from around sandwiches. She takes their rubbish to the short loud bins.

> the lines on the backs
> of their thighs
> below their blue and white
> school dresses
> are red
> striated
> when they stand
> their skin is music stave
> letter practice
> repetition
> when they stand
> their skin
> is read

Bella is the only one her sister will speak to when she wets herself at school. Four. Her sister is four and has started school early and believes everything she is told. When she is told she is not allowed to ask to go to the toilet in class time because she should have done that at lunch she holds and squirms and squirms and holds and then feels hot wet the trickle down her leg the puddle on her little red plastic chair and she stands and she runs to the toilets and goes in and locks the door and won't come out.

>   grey everything is
>   grey and why is it always so cold
>   in the blue mountains
>   where we are without our mum
>   and the door will not keep enough out

Bella is called from her class where she is learning how many days are in each month (all the rest have thirty-one except for February alone) and she goes to the toilets and drops to the cold tiled floor and slither scoots under the door. She undresses then dresses her sister who will speak to no one else. Spare clothes that the teacher has handed her: blue corduroy overalls, a white t-shirt with orange flowers, a scratchy green jumper. No socks. Her sister spends the rest of the day with bare feet inside her moist shoes. But she does come out, holding Bella by the hand, pigtails skewed from the jumper being pulled down over her head, her ankles showing, her fingers bluish from the cold.

>   we keep each other
>   nested in the cold
>   we spill stories in the night
>   light-filled
>   we keep each other
>   full

FRANCIS: Francis is the name she chooses for herself when she is twelve. I didn't give you middle names, her mother says. I thought you'd rather choose them for yourselves. She tasted the name it sounded like books like Narnia like Mr Tumnus might show up sweltering in a Sydney summer, his parasol no match for the sun. Francis is the name she calls herself; she tries and fails to get others to say it aloud so at night, under her blue and white striped sheet, two fingers inside herself, pushing at her own edges, she whispers it, after her sister has gone to sleep.

                                          she couldn't go deep
                                                         enough
                                        it didn't matter how hard she
                                                         pushed
                                         she couldn't stretch wide
                                                         enough
                                            couldn't fit enough in
                                                    bone traced
                                          fingers without length
                                          the way it feels to never
                                                   have enough
                                                          reach

STEVIE: She picks Stevie because of Stevie Smith. Because her *Novel on Yellow Paper* (1937) is the spine on her mother's bookshelf that always draws her eye. She doesn't read it, but she takes the name, insistently. She will make them say it. She will force the name down and out of her loved one's throats. Her friends do. They take the name up with glee. But her sister and her mother refuse. So at school, she is Stevie. Stevie is black eyeliner for lipstick her lips turning her mouth into a red wet cavern lined by a matt night sky. She is thick black tights, stolen silver rings on every finger and each thumb, doc marten boots. She is open-wide take on anyone terrified under tough. She reads Sylvia Plath who writes *the blood jet is poetry* and one night, walking down an alley in Erskineville, she learns how to bruise bleed her knuckles by slamming her left fist into fences and walls.

                                               blood doesn't jet
                                                        it seeps
                                                 it leaves traces
                                         on brick, on iron, on wood
                                                     it pushes up

>   through the bandage weave
>   it holds the wound
>   redly open
>   it congeals and remembers
>   night alley the thunk of
>   the body against surfaces
>   that do not give

RAYNE: This name, she takes for anonymity, for disappearing, for the way that heroin turns each day grey. Rayne is only comfortable when she's emptied out. She is legs spread for her lover, she is arm open always to the wind, to steel. She is what she can sell next (books, leather chaps, saxophone, flute, mobile phone, oil paints, herself).

>   morning is hunt sell buy
>   acrid powder sizzle
>   shoot
>   shoot the day
>   find love
>   find nearness
>   find warmth
>   try to read
>   to write
>   to make a story
>   from abject fluid
>   from wanting
>   from what a room looks
>   like coming
>   down

PERSEPHONE: Persephone lives in Rayne she is the dungeon worker she treads through room after room; a magic box that holds her in while men knock at the door and ask her for everything. Persephone is the name the men say without irony. Come here, lay down over my knees, don't call out, no one will come, be still, don't struggle, but moan.

SARAH: Sarah lives after Persephone. After rooms with no daylight after being always held. Down. Sarah lives in a different series of rooms plastered with mirrors and on the bed, too many towels. She uses and washes and uses and washes and hangs red white red white red white blue towels. Sarah is lingerie and wobbling in heels, she is open, she is waiting for money, for men to get off her, for the way her body feels after the weight of them is gone.

Rayne is keeper and kept. She is trying-to-write. She takes a huge clay cup of peppermint tea and a cigarette out to the overgrown garden and balances a journal on her lap. She imagines what it would be like, to write. To make text. She picks up her pen. She writes that she is trying to write. She smokes. Tea turns her throat hot. She writes that she wishes she could write. In the garden she thinks about Persephone and Sarah and imagines them gone.

>
> from over the fence the sound
> of a kettle
> boiled
> from over the fence the sound
> of a life without
> a magic box
> of rooms
> from over the fence the sound
> of a person with only
> one name

KARINA: Karina is detox with two garbage bags of clothes and a set of juggling clubs and enough money from her mother for three phone calls measured out in twenty-cent pieces.

> under the shower
> is where the body
> finds relief
> the hot sting of water
> pelts
> and washes bile
> spit
> shit
> away
> under the shower
> she stares at the open
> hole in her arm
> and sings her dealer's
> phone number
> but he doesn't
> come

Karina is meetings, meetings, meetings. There is a script that they follow and it comforts and terrifies simultaneously. God. The word, the thing, the naming, the grappling, the trying to let in. It takes her ten years to refuse higher power, divine intervention, being kept clean by a beneficent being. It takes her ten years to move out of all of those rooms, filled with circles of people, helping each other to get or to stay clean. And then? Karina is writing.

> when no god decides
> which bus she will catch
> who lies flayed

                    on an open road
              while others sail past
                            to lunch
                             to work
                             to home
                     no god decides
              which name she takes
          what person that name makes
                     no god decides
             which words she places
                 for you to read here

MAMA: Mama is who comes next. Made in the blunt vice of birth, through muscle and blood and milk and bone. Made in the sound of her children's voices saying her name, in playgrounds, next to change tables, on her knees picking up toast crusts and mandarin segments. Made in the dark, in nights of nodding off in a breastfeeding chair, sleeping while her babies sleep. Made in grimace, and frustration, and come-here-go-away: in love.

                             bitten
                     these children
                               want
                       to tear her
                              apart
                  then put her back
                           together
                         they bang
                       their bodies
                       against hers
                         they grab
                               hair

                                                          lip
                                                          ear
                                                they push pull
                                         they insist she notice
                                                     everything

When her oldest boy is two-and-a-half, and her youngest isn't even crawling yet, she tries to get them both out of the house. The baby is dressed and changed, she has a bag packed with rusks and water and fruit and spare nappies, but the toddler is still in his pyjamas. Stripy. Cotton warm. Cosy from the night. She has his clothes in her hands, she is asking for him to come closer so she can take off his pjs and put on his pants (one leg, two legs!) but he runs. He runs from her and the baby starts to cry and he laughs and runs and laughs so hard he gets the hiccups and she is saying please please please please.

                                              when babies cry
                                         the world telescopes
                                                         down
                                              to that one wail
                                         to needing it to stop
                                                  to be solved
                                                   to be quiet
                                                 when babies
                                                           cry
                                             nipples leak milk
                                    and although there's nothing
                                                        wrong
                                                it is all wrong
                                                 when babies
                                                           cry

>   there is no
>   way
>   out

She stops trying to get him to come voluntarily and instead grabs him as he runs past. The baby is still crying. She pulls off his stripy warm pants. He is struggling. He yells no, repeatedly. She asks him to step into his jeans (one leg, two legs!) but he will not. He pulls against her. The baby is still crying. He pushes at her. Crying. She picks him up and tries to pull his pants on that way, while he is in the air. He struggles and yells. Crying. She yells, her voice a desperate loud wobble, please help me! And then she drops him. She doesn't realise he is quite so far from the ground. He doesn't land on his feet. They slip out from under him and he falls, his head smacking against the floorboards. They all cry. She tries to hold him and the baby. She says sorry. A year later, he finally forgets.

>   forged
>   she is forged
>   by her children
>   by the whitered
>   flashes
>   of rage
>   by the endlessness
>   of days
>   by the way they sleep
>   unfolded
>   their lips
>   plumped
>   their legs
>   splayed
>   by the drawings they make

                                                             bubble belly
                                                          sticks for arms
                                                          never a neck
                                                     enormous grins
                                   made from a single line
                             this is you mama they say
                                                            this is you

QUINN: Quinn comes after the first book is written, after the hysterectomy the surgeon said she had to have (fast growing fibroid, vascular, the weight above her cervix, incontinence), after she couldn't stay at one end of the gender binary anymore. Quinn takes her last name as her first, but keeps her whole name for her writing, for her work. Her partner says I can't call you that. It's too harsh. Her friends and colleagues try to remember, and some of them do better than others. Her children call her Mama, or Mum, or Karina, or Dr Mama. In the beginning it feels important for all of them to call her by her next chosen name, but she doesn't insist. She waits. She writes. She slides. She pauses the hunt for the next name. She takes them all. She is PK/Francis/Stevie/Rayne/Persephone/Sarah/Mama/Karina/Quinn. She takes them all and holds them inside her skin. She is all names, for herself: she is no one named.

                                           body under blanket
                                              gaps in gums
                                                   gone
                                   the mattress is
                                         off the floor
                                          the children
                                               unfold
                                  writing is written
                                    baths are taken

                                                               each name
                                                                  holds
                                                                 its own

It is this calling, this naming, that changes she to he. Because Quinn is the name that is next, that is last. Quinn takes his last name for his first and for a while, has only one name. His friends begin to remember. His children do too. When he tells them he isn't a girl anymore the littlest one says
    'Can I still call you Mama?' and Quinn pulls him onto his knee and says 'Yes, of course'.
    'But now you're a boy Mama?'
    'Now I'm a boy Mama' Quinn says, adding this new name to the list. The sixteen-year relationship does not survive because the changing of the name is a shell that holds the changing of a pronoun, the changing of a body, the shining bright terror of stepping somewhere new, and the relationship can't survive this. He is stepping too far. She wants to stay. He finds a last name. Eades. His grandmother's maiden name. A name that rolls perfectly from Quinn. A name that holds its own. A name that steps past all the other names, that has its feet in dirt and its face in the orange-hearted sun, that is flat-chested and deep-voiced, that writes and writes and knows now how to appear.

Sources
Cixous, H. (1991). *'Coming to writing' and other essays.* Cambridge, Massachusetts: Harvard University Press, p. 2.
Irigaray, L. (2002). *To speak is never neutral* (G. Schwab, Trans.). London: Continuum, p. 7.
Plath, S. (1963). Kindness. In T. Hughes (Ed.), *Sylvia Plath: collected poems.* Great Britain: Faber and Faber Limited.
Smith, S. (1937). *Novel on yellow paper: or, Work it out for yourself.* New York: Morrow.

Under Them

Shine on me

I left home when I was 16. Bipolar mother. Sadness in doorways. Too much of not enough. I left home when I was 16 and I went to live in a refuge, and in the refuge I learnt how to make homemade tattoos with India ink and needles, and how to smoke, and sniff aerosols, and how to carry myself like a wound. I learnt that I had nothing. I slept with a chest of drawers against my bedroom door because Wendy, in the room next to me, said she was going to shave my eyebrows off in the night. I lost my virginity with the girl upstairs in my single bed. She bled on me and the sheets. I sat in the courtyard and smoked. I went to school. I drew the angriest pictures in the world. I knew loneliness better than I knew my own skin. I wanted to sleep, and sleep, and sleep. Everything I was, was emptiness and sleep.

I had been there for about a year when one of my mum's ex-girlfriends decided I was going off the rails. She thought boarding school would be the best thing for me, and I agreed. Eight weeks later I was in a bunk bed at Sydney's cheapest boarding school. I arrived already tattooed, with a half shaved head and scars on my wrists. I arrived with one suitcase holding everything I owned, to a school full of Catholic girls. They were country. I was city. They were ducks and liberty print and moleskins. I was doc boots and Jane's Addiction t-shirts and torn jeans. They were oboes. I was electric guitar. We eyed each other off in the common room. I made friends with the smokers, and found a place there.

I joined the choir. I still wanted to sleep. I went to art classes. I still wanted to sleep. It was much easier to get out of boarding school than it was to get out of the refuge, and I spent most weekends drunk and stoned at other people's houses. But I went to choir practice. And one day, the teacher taught us a song.

> *Shine on me, shine on me. Let the light, from the lighthouse, shine on me.*

We sang it in low harmony. We sang it in the music room, on green carpet, music stands surrounding us, fluorescent lights humming. We sang it and the words settled in on me. We sang. We sang and from the song, for a brief moment, I felt something. I felt greater than the sum of my parts. I felt strong. I felt like I could shed my homeless skin. I felt like I could survive.

We sang the song for a month and moved on.

I forgot about it. I finished school, and went to Uni. I aimed at bravery, and tried to write. I played in bands, and got more tattoos, and studied Foucault. And then I met her.

Did I know she was a junkie? Probably. I had always been drawn to thin people in black clothes. I fell in love. I used. I slept. I ran out of money, fast. I stole things. I worked in dungeons and brothels, and sold almost every book I owned. I had managed to keep a handful: Winterson's *Art and Lies*, a complete works of Shakespeare, my *Norton Anthology of Poetry*, Atwood's *The Handmaid's Tale* were among them. But then our dealer told us if we didn't pay him what we owed him we'd never score from him again. And I had to pack my last precious bag of books, and walk up to Newtown to sell them. And she was standing next to me at the traffic lights, and it started to rain, and I felt a surging rage from underneath the smack.

"What are we going to do?"

"We'll just get clean"

And I knew she was lying. And I sold the books, in the rain, and we paid the dealer, and I left her. I went to detox and rehab, and a halfway house. Flesh grew on my bones. I met the woman I stayed with for sixteen years. I imagined that I might be allowed to do more than survive.

Ten years later, wanting children was the most daring thing I could do. To have survived, and then to think that I could hold and have and keep something so bright and sweet and new; this was my terrible hope. And as I planned, and hoped, and dreamt, I sang.

> *Let the light, from the lighthouse, shine on me.*

And they came. Those boys who say 'look at me I'm a poppy', and 'mama', and 'I love you'. Those boys who don't know about dark rooms and needles and sleep like death. Those boys who dragged me out into the day, who let me keep them alive, who insist on wakefulness, on love.

They know the song. I've sung it to them since they were born. They ask me to sing it to them sometimes, and let me hold them and rock them as I do. They don't usually sing along.

But there's this: winter solstice. Benji's arms around my neck, so soft they nearly melt into my collar bones. I have my right arm behind my back, supporting his body while I piggy back him. Zach's hand in my other hand. The balancing act of two children. Sal is there, and we walk. We walk, and I start singing. There are hundreds of people, in the dark, walking, with pink and purple and yellow and orange lanterns.

> *Shine on me. Shine on me.*

And as I walk I know this: not only that these children are the best of me, but that I am the best of them. I walk in my shining skin, gold dust in my hair, the light of a thousand lanterns tracing the darkness and confusing the stars, and my children sing with me. Those piping voices, my cracking notes.

> *Let the light, from the lighthouse, shine on me.*

Promise

Exhausted.
Leaking.
The slump produced by a stare that
humps my back and makes
elbows ache. Lines of
mortar across the road
a beaming demand.
Notice the brick
work.
Symmetry.
The smugness of straight lines.
The tram. The tram that will
carry me later
into the fuzzy city full
of decorations and oranges
slung like baubles from beams.
The tram waits and I slump.
Into coffee into how
will I write again
into pull yourself together
into stop leaking stop looking at lines
of mortar like they mean something.
Anything.
I promised to write a poem a day.
I promised.

This Mother Thing

I maintain that I do not have to leave
the house at night
all leathery and eyelinered,
all booted up and raw.

I maintain that I do not miss those
smoky rooms (wait that's not allowed any more)
where we strut and, without looking,
compare tattoos.

Because two years ago I had you.
You with your blonde hair shining, your eyes
like a creek after rain, that vein
that's so blue on the side of your small nose
that people think you've been bruised.

Because two years ago you came
out of me and landed here and grew.

There is no going out. We (she and me) wash
and cook and wash and clean and love.

This mother thing is the making of me but I miss
those pulsing rooms,
the feel of all of you
pressing in
on all of me.

Milkling

I am watching you grow the skin on your
lips. The sucking blister has come
and gone three times, a white amulet
of skin peeling and then
disappearing.

Do you swallow it when you suck? I see
the peak of your upper lip get tougher
each time and soon the sucking will have no
effect. Your lips will be thicker for new skin.
They will not blister.

Your belly button was a spiral, and then a c.
When it was still healing over, the place
that joined you to me, I would sometimes get
an alarming glimpse, of redness, a moistened
opening, and imagined it tunneling
all the way
to the centre
of you.

It goes too fast. Suddenly I understand
the women who talk about treasuring
dawn feeds. Those women have other children
and so this is the only time for gazing.

I would gaze if I could but instead I hang above you
slack jawed while you suck and smile
your milkling smiles. Somehow, even in semi-sleep,
my arms keep a sure hold of you.

You are warm against my belly and we smell
of each other.

I could be tangled here
and not let go. But I do, and I ache
for separateness.

And every day I can't wait
to descend into brief sleep.

And every day I drag my feet
to try and slow it all down,
this exquisite entanglement
which is not enough
and too much
all
at the same
time.

The wanting house

The kettle is still warm from the last
time it was boiled. My palm catches heat
from its metal hide. I fill it from
the copper tap. Golden arc. Joni
Mitchell sings from the hallway. Blue.

Outside it is cold. Spring is here but it is not.
The heat pack around my neck presses
at my shoulders and I can smell wheat and green velvet
and the pain of a decade old injury
that will not leave, no matter what I do.

Outside it is cold. In here I write,
and boil the kettle again, for tea.
For heat. For the sound of something happening.
The industriousness of water changing form.
The boil. Tea. Heat. Wheat. Write.
Drink while music winds its way
through the damp air (songs are like tattoos).

The phone rings. Everything is gone.
I am in a house that holds six hearts beating
when it is full. I am in a house that is copper
and wheat pack and this page of text. I am in
a house that is empty. I am in a house that
wants, like it's missing its own skin, to gather
up those beating hearts and hold them
inside its beating walls. I am in a house
that threads its desire through the cold,
that sends its wants out, under doors and over
windowsills.

This house knows me. It needs certain
things: poetry, the sound of our children
in the mornings before the sun has risen, toast
crumbs on its floorboards; everyday dreams.

The heat pack is cooling. The tea is drunk. The
copper tap drips. Joni wishes she had a river
she could skate away on. The place between
my shoulder blades that is weak and has no
name asks for more heat, for a gentle hand. I
keep writing.

Creek Walk

My mother and I write letters to each other.
We resort to pen and paper in the hope that the time it takes
for the mail to arrive will slow our stinging words. No email this.

In between letters I think
about what to tell her, and how.

We walk the creek, he and I in the
cold, bright wind. It is Autumn. The weather
is changing, and I can feel this change on my skin.
His cheeks are cold, and big, and red. On
his head a hand-knitted beanie that arrived
one day in the post. I could almost see
those hands of yours at the needles,
the way you would loop the wool over with a deft pinky swipe.

And out of your gums your teeth come glistening. Not like
pearls, but something sharper, like pincers, like claws, like
knives.

There is a dead cat, hairless, headless,
lying prone on the Merri creek path.
Stiffly skinned. I think about how a head
would look, digested.

When we get home I decide to bury
the placenta – it has been defrosted for this moment.
I expect love but find instead the gag from leaking
bits of blood onto the brick.

The animals gather, Penny licking.
The burying, the gagging, the burying.

Ant line

I awake with your skull
resting in the cup of my eye
socket. I cannot escape the
feeling that one movement of
yours will break the bones of my face.

You breathe.

I make quiet attempts
to manoeuvre out
       from underneath
you. Your skull presses resolutely down.
I have not felt anything heavier. Ever.

You wake up. You notice ants
and honey drops. You want toast
with no crumbs. *No crumbs*, you say,
insistently, as if I am made of magic,
as if I can force cooked bread
not to lose parts of itself.

You are determined not
to leave a trail. You don't like
ants. The smell they make when crushed.
Not knowing which species are
biters, which ones are sugar seekers.
Which ones seek out our creases, to
crawl amongst. No crumbs. No crumbs.

This is how I know you: by
your hands, the way you
move them through air, those
imitative gestures that come along
when you most want something.

This is how I know you: by
the aching in your voice when you
say please, by your hip wiggle, the way
you land when you fall.

When you fall. And grit presses itself
into your knees. And skin leaves the
heels of your hands. And the sun holds
the side of your face, and
suddenly you are seraphim: a breathing,
angelic
thing.

You are love's splintering heart. You
are a shining, a single
moment in time, an idea in the back
yard one August afternoon,
the capturing of a life, like
dust, like honey, like crumbs
followed by ants, avoiding the crush
of fingers, waiting to sting, and chatter skitter,
to gather in flickering groups around globes of sugar
that shine, in the sun of your eye brought up close.

Big things break

You are nearly five. I am on the train
to the city and there are electric guitars and rasping voices coming
through my headphones. The rain is clearing. I look up
and see the skywheel has its pods.
And I remember you.

Eight weeks old.
Black Saturday fires.
It was so hot the skywheel
cracked. Metal buckling until it could not sustain its own weight.
When we went outside I felt as if the air was going to catch,
as if we were breathing
in fire. As if it was not possible to survive.

And that was in the city. It was not Kinglake. There were no embers
in the wind. But dust. So much dust and wind and the cracking
skywheel and my breastmilk
stained singlets and you so hot you could barely
move.

All you could do was drink. I had a two litre bottle
of water with me always. You were upending me. You were tipping me
sideways. You were unending in all of the ways where you got
exactly what it was you needed while I dripped and grazed
through the squalling
days.

And now you are nearly five. And the skywheel
has its pods. They sit against the blue Melbourne
sky and wait to carry thousands into the view. They are
ready to be fulfilled; to be empty, and then
full.

Pinwheeled spinnakers rotating in all kinds of wind,
they are finally the vessels that will show us
buildings like gleaming spines, that will hold onto the shouts
of children and then caress them
later, in the unturning night, like newly made marbles
or things made from sapphires and gold.

When we go past the skywheel next week, on the Bolte Bridge, its pillars
holding back gulls and shipping containers and the iron red cranes
that make us think of dinosaurs you will notice and say
    Look the skywheel is finished and
    how much does it cost and
    can we go on it and
    tell me again about the fires and
    why was it so extremely incredibly hot and
    how can it be so hot that something that big can break?
And I will try to answer all of your questions, the way I do, and say
    yes and
    a lot and
    probably and
    you were eight weeks old and
    it was so hot that the skywheel could not sustain its own weight.

Metal melts. Hard things are soft. Small things get big. Big things break.

Lay down, lay down

The floorboards have had enough
of being walked on. They are trodden through,
they are worn. They wait impatiently for all of us
to leave so they can sigh, and rest, and feel the
weight of rugs and furniture and dust, pressing
lightly along their lengths, like love.

The beds are sick of being slept in. They are
claustrophobic. They are colonised by dust mites
and skin flakes and sweat. They dream of a night
alone, with nothing between them and the air but
a sheet. The imprints of bodies remain because
there's nothing they can do about the way weight
changes the form of their mattresses, over time, with love.

The couch doesn't want to be sat on. It is bowed
and exhausted. Its cushions are flattened and huffy.
Last night one of the children spilt a whole cup
of milk onto its seat. White river, there was an attempt at
escape. There was an attempt at repelling, but eventually
the cow juice settled into its creases, damply, with love.

The table is tired of holding things up. Food, especially,
but also cutlery, and those plates with roses on them.
It is fed up with being accidentally drawn on, and then
the scouring that follows. It despises the way it is
moved when the floor is mopped, and resents elbows and
the small feet that dance on its top, with love.

The walls are sick of holding up the roof. The roof
is sick of holding out the sky. The tiles are sick
of stopping the birds from making their nests. The windows
are fed up with keeping out the rain. The stumps are tired
of lifting the house up out of the dirt. The front door
has had enough of keeping strangers out. The lights are tired
of being light. The taps have had enough of letting water in.
The toilet is sick of taking water (and everything else) out.
The bath is fed up with all the cleaning and bathing. The fucking
soap that rimes its edge and slither slips along its bottom
as if it belongs there, as if it is home.

The curtains are exhausted at the thought of being drawn,
the chairs cannot bear to keep their legs straight,
the kettle refuses to whistle,
the oven will not get hot,
the shower has dried up,
the bathroom tiles, finally, surrender to mould
and the mould grows. The mould is blue and bottle green,
and a sick, bright orange that flares in the corners.

The house lays itself down. It sighs. Relief. Surrender.
Dust. Mould. Scum. Mites. The busyness of ants.
Lay down, lay down, lay down.
Let yourself be coated.
This. This is love.

Always going home (a domestic cycle)
1. Give (I cannot be separate)

It is almost unbearable,
the nearness of these children. The feeling
that they are trying to swallow me.
I want more than anything to be
out, and away,
and at exactly the same time I cannot bear
to leave them, so
soft, so beaming beautiful
shining like silver underwater shot
by the sun. At exactly the same time
I want them to climb back
inside of me, and I into them, as if
we could consume each other, as if
our bodies have never been entirely
separate. As if we are made of dough,
and by pushing into each other, we will
incorporate; we will mix.
We will be made into a new thing full
of air and yeast and warmth. The space
between us elastic with give.

2. A nowhere place
(I remember that you are here)

Green beans surrender
their tops and tails. There is music
from somewhere else, guitar
plucked and a woman's voice low
and sad. I come upon you
in the nowhere place between
kitchen and bathroom, outside
our toddler's door. The plucked
strings and sad voice have settled
somewhere under my ribs
and I almost have trouble
breathing I am so stained
by melancholy. Thirteen years.

You take me in your arms, the nowhere
place enough for holding, and the smell
of your skin is exactly
as it should be. From the kitchen
the brown of roasting meat and hunks
of sweet potato. Starch caramelising
in spite of the dread weight of anxiety.
Burnt sugar crackles on the oven tray. You turn
the music off. I never think to do that,
I say.

The nowhere place is where all
the important things happen in our house.
Most shouts start here. Resistance lives just outside
the bathroom door. This is the place
where our children turn to jelly, or rockets, or
limpets, or clowns, or raging red things
with wide open mouths and instant tears.

Most hurried 'are you ok?' moments happen here.
Sometimes these are said with care, sometimes
they are a thrown accusation. Arguments wait
for months, next to the cupboard that holds our towels.
These are the arguments about small things,
that end up being big things, that are never
about small things.

The nowhere place is where we dance. A child in
each of our arms, 'family dance time!', we yell.
And then it is the four of us wiggling and spinning,
holding on and letting go, winding out and winding in.
It doesn't take long before it's over,
and we spool back to different corners of the house,
where less important things are waiting.

So when you find me in the nowhere place,
and stop, on your way to the washing line,
to hold me, and I can smell the aching sweetness
of your skin, just for that moment
there is no raging toddler
in the other room, or a demand
from our older child to jump, now, over
this red piece of string. There is only
our nowhere place and the smells
of home, of you, holding me.

3. The bus home
(I am drawn back in)

The cows with their heads
down; the work of it, all
that grass. To have to
continue eating even
after the sun has gone
down.

Rain in the
distance, grey wall, clouds
letting out all that
they hold, making good
on their damp promise.

Headlights. Guitar and
harp. A woman's voice.

300 kilometres away those boys
of mine are in pyjamas
eating apple and making
dinosaur noises and I
can't work out if I'm glad
for the closing distance or not.

What comes closer is this:
Love. Chaos. Crying in the night.
Food thrown like a missile.
Seeing up close how language starts.

No. This. Want. Donkey.
Love.

And in the time
it has taken me to write
this we have passed
through the wall
of rain.

The clouds have
drawn themselves in. The
cows still eat.

The kilometres
disappear, and I understand
there is no choice. I will always
go home again.

I will always
be this: Mother. Poet. Climbing
frame. Cook. Tissue. Pack Horse.
Cuddler. Lover. Loved. This.

4. What happens on the other side of the world (I almost split)

This feeling needs a poem, is what I thought, lying
in my epsom salted bath, as if the water
might bring me home. As if the heat and wet
would call me back from where I had been.

I am here, but I am not. Some part of me is
still on that hill in Montmarte, a man
in grey trousers playing Cohen's 'Hallelujah'
on the steps of the cathedral, surrounded by Parisians
warmed by notes and the sun, and the way his face
and hands worked, effortlessly, at the song.

Some part of me is still in that Hackney café where it took
an hour to bring breakfast, but we told stories
in the noise at that thick communal table and drank
coffee and I was not six hands, three hearts, coated in questions;
the extreme luxury of sitting still.

Some part of me is still standing alone on the platform
at Paddington station, snow falling through the parabolic roof,
hands colder than they've ever been, grinning gormlessly up
at the steel rucked sky.

I am not automaton here: I did get off the plane. You were all there,
at the airport, a welcome home poster held between you,
awake far too late. You covered me in kisses, I leaked tears
at the sight of you, I was heartsick and glad. So three nights later
when you said 'maybe you didn't want to come home' and I leapt
off the couch as if I'd been stung it was only the truth of it,
biting at me. I was hurt, I told you.

Didn't you know how much I'd missed all of you, all of this:
the yellow kitchen table,
the shadows of Callistemons, being woken every morning
with the word Mummy, eating dinner half standing, in puddles
of spilt water and pieces of carrot ... the love.

By the end I felt as though another dinner alone, in Paris, was
unbearable. I retreated to the hotel and drank tea with
long life milk—pungent and wrong. By the end I felt
as though I was rent in two. But there's this. I am only half here.

Part of me is still back there, the dust of Le Louvre on my boots, coffee
warm in my hands, testing new words, writing madly on the Metro,
walking the Seine, so cold I could only be awake. Part of me is
still childless, and a writer, and single, and living in Paris and London.
Part of me is making my way there, even as I wipe honey
from my hands and beg my four year old to put pants on,
and discuss zombies and super powers, and how to break the rules
of gravity.

This unbearable split.

The bath, it seems, is not enough. I will continue convincing myself.
I will keep reeling myself back in.
This is the life I have; that is some other woman's life,
who feels lonely sometimes, but mostly has bright
cold air in her lungs, and space, and lovers for days,
and a small London flat where she makes tea just the way she likes it,
and writes.

This unbearable split.
My waterlogged skin.
No. This. Want.
Mother.
Poet.
We.

Small children do not splash or cry out

Zach was always careful in the bath. He was careful everywhere. This is a child who didn't walk until he was twenty-one months old. He walked, but only if he was holding onto something: me, a trolley, a wall. Zach was always careful in the bath, even with me in there with him (and I was with him most of the time). Sometimes he'd forget himself, the warm water leaching caution from his limbs, and lunge, and slip. I was always there to catch, and say

> I gotcha honey.

> I gotcha, he'd repeat. I gotcha.

Then he'd stand, caution reinstated, and play his careful tipping games. When he was twenty-three months old I was seven months pregnant with Benji and it was hard to fit both of us in there. I stayed out and he played alone. I was watching. Then I turned to get his toothbrush and when I turned around there he was. Lying down along the enamel bottom, water covering his wide-open eyes. No moving. No thrashing. No trying to push his face up and out of the inch of water between him and breath. Those brown eyes, water covered, staring straight up, like the ceiling was the last thing he would ever see. It's true that time is elastic, it concertinas, it opens and closes: it breathes. I grabbed his little arm and pulled him up, up, out. He took one huge breath and then screamed into my shoulder, all wet terror and clinging. I was watching. I had turned.

They told me I would be able to pick his cry out, that I would know my baby in a crowded room. How? All babies looked and sounded the same. I was terrified, after he was born, of not recognising him. The sameness of infants when you haven't had one yet yourself. I dreamt again and again of walking in to a room full of babies and being unable to pick him out. Too many cheeks and sucking blisters. Fine hair. Turning heads.

That squalling sound: less like birds and more like night things, sucking creatures, half vampire half faerie, all need. Or that I had found him, but when I got home it was not him: I had taken the wrong baby. My baby was alien but he was my alien. Now this: doubled alien, drinking my milk as if it belonged to him, the thick wedge of his tongue pushing out as I came near. The other pregnant dream I had more than once was this: being able to take him out, and then put him back in. All I had to do was reach between my legs, put two fingers inside myself, pinch an errant foot between them and pull. What I held was a tiny, perfect, baby. No blood. But with translucent skin and gills still. Gills that could somehow breathe air as well as amniotic fluid. Sal and I would look him over, then I'd make sure the umbilical cord was untangled, and poke him back in.

And now this (it is not a dream). Twelve weeks old at the most. Pre-eclampsia and induction meant he was thin, undercooked, all scrawn and ribs and jaundice. Thin thighs. He cried in shifts. Between one and three hours. Sal and I took it in turns to rock him while the other one of us lay in dread, not sleeping, waiting for the minutes to turn. Twenty minutes on, twenty minutes off. Was it the tiredness that had me imagining his small death? We had a tiny shower, two glass walls, a shower tray that if you blocked the drain with a washer, or your thigh, would hold about ten centimetres of water. No bath (it was before we moved to the house with the copper taps, the yellow enamel, all those bricks, the Callistemons). Sometimes, in the yawning day (because time is like breath) I would have a shower. It was an activity for us, like pram walks and tummy time. There was the undressing and dressing, busyness, blessed movement, and in between, this: water. My back against the lime scaled glass, thigh become plug. The sound of the shower tray filling. The way Zach would press his whole body into mine, clinging limpet rockling darling downy goosling lost against my chest. Stinging water dreaming warmth me singing *take these broken wings and learn to fly, all your life,*

you were only waiting for this moment to arise.

It made a beautiful picture. My voice. The water. His curling trust. But in my head I was doing this: laying him down in the shower tray and watching as the water rose, tickling at his ears, then covering his cheeks, pooling over his eyes, entering his mouth and nose. It's not that I wanted him gone: it was that I couldn't go on. I couldn't go on but there was no choice. What really happened was this: I kept singing. He kept curling.

Blackbird, fly. Blackbird, fly. Into the arms of the dark black night.

The hot water ran out. He screamed and arched, alive, all reaction. I braced my lower back and stood, turning off the ice. I got a towel over both of us and shushed and hushed him to the bedroom. Stood naked and dripping over him, made sure he was dry and nappied and warm and clothed, then dried and dressed myself. Kept going.

Away With Them

Shiver

Heat. Heat that takes
and holds and spills.

Heat that turns
breath to a gasp.

At the Siam Paragon shopping centre
we wait for the doors to open,

for cold air cold drinks ice-cream
prickling skin flinching against change.

We sit at the edge
of a fountain and the kids

lean and dip their hands in,
and draw

pictures that dry
as soon as they're laid down on cement.

A man two metres away settles
a parboiled pig's head

onto a shrine for elephants and
shoos away the pigeons that come to peck, daily, at flesh.

Incense laces the muggy morning.
The pigeons hunt pork.

The children moan at the day.
The doors open.

Cold. Cold, we step in.
Cold, and the children shiver

delicious and don't think
about the afternoon that will come, full of mosquito bitten sun.

Sequined

In the morning, when
it is still dark and
not even the birds
are awake, when we
have tried everything,
everything, and the
children will not go back
to sleep, I remember
the torches. I give
one to each of them.

The curtains are covered
in sequins. And so they make stars.

The torches shine
shimmer shunt
the light out to walls,
ceiling, faces, floor.

There is light all around
in the dark dark
morning and we picnic
on the bed because
hotel breakfasts are
never early enough.

Cashews. Grapes. A floury
peach. Half a stale croissant
each. We eat. The torches
shine. The sequins are
still stars. The day begins.

Three nights in Kanchanaburi
1. What we want them to see

Air-conditioned bus ride. We
all sleep—grateful, curled, hanging
off edges, cool.

When we arrive there are fans too loud
to talk above, and iced tea that drops the heat
from our throats.

The children jump on bamboo couches and knock over the tea.
I try not to want them gone.

They fight over torn digimon
cards and whose ice-cream is
better while giant orange
millipedes limber slither
past their feet and herds
of butterflies move over their heads and
we find ourselves saying over and over

    Look. Look. Look.

These boys of ours, who fall one on each side of the divide.

Who notice or don't. Who stop or keep moving. Who rarely meet.

    Look. Look. Look.

We ache for synchronicity.

For the double intake of breath.

For the moment that will grab
them both and make them pause.

There is no forcing it. There is no making them meet.

2. What we carry

On the second day
in the unfocus of my ten pm eyes
the headlights behind us are orbs,
are beamed halos, rain traced, light magic:
grace.

Warm air. Slipping mud.
Sleepy children at our sides.
Noodle bellies.
Chili tongues.

The way tiredness and damp
air make all of our bodies soft slippery slide,
unending touch.

We drive through the night and carry
with us from the day these things:
Elephant hide.
Dust.
Waterfalls.
Nibbling fish.
The heat.
Piggybacking the littlest one for
so long that his belly slid
over my back, like we had
tipped a bucket of water
between us.

Risky ice but we didn't care.
Sticky rice—the surprise of our
white toast honey licking kid unwrapping
the green banana leaf parcel and

pulling off a piece to eat, then
taking the whole thing.
Mine, he said.

Death Railway. Trying not
to barter at the site of so much
gone wrong. The kids insisting
on buying bamboo swords, the racketing
rails, leather seats, high wind,
war-dead lacing the air with memory,
with story, with nothing, with us.

All this, in the tuk tuk, going back to the hotel,
in the rain, in the night, carried with us on our skins
like we might never forget how it feels to be
so close to the dead, and so dearly loved.

3. How we climb

On the third day we are brave
and we go to temples. We think
they won't manage. We prepare
to split up.

The taxi with the open sides and red
and blue walls pulls in
to the temple and we see the mouth
of a dragon halfway up a mountain.

The steps are its ridged and keening tongue.
The kids want to climb, to beat flesh, to step inside saliva,
to reach teeth base of throat belly tail's end thrum.

The kids want to climb, so we do.

We do, and we anticipate this: our five year old
cringer heart whinger whenever he hits
a heartbeat
from moving
won't do it, can't do it,
will fall
or sink
or flop
or stop.

We climb. We climb and he climbs.
Knees bend. Ankles flex. Centipedes are crunched
under sandals with joy, and eventually, intent.

The three year old stops at a platform halfway
to ring bells. Enough, he says, enough.

But the other kid goes. Knees. Ankles. Centipedes. We are
rung forward, the brass hides of bells sending us up. We push
through sun over ridge rock past bush no one left but us we push up.

'I just keep moving my legs,' he says
like it's a revelation.
And it is.

This from the kid who didn't walk
until he was two.
This from the kid who trips and
tumbles on flat ground, shoelaces tied.

Who says he wishes the whole world was inside.

At the top he puts a stone in
his pocket to take home, a piece of
the place he found.

At the top it is building rubble, a blue rope, broken tiles, and what we can see.

He doesn't care what he finds.
At the top he wants to know that he can get there.
At the top he wants to take a piece home.

More

Lychees eaten off branches
bought from the market.
Bursting prickled plumped
squirt they fill, each one of them,
the cavity that is my mouth.

Black seed spat, bark skin dropped
back into the bay. The leaves that
I forage amongst to get more.
The children refuse to try them. Eyeballs
they say, too slippery, they don't like fruit
that is grey.

I forage and pluck and pull and squirt.

Lychees prickle barked squint as I tear
of the skins are all.
For me.

The resort

The resort kills poems.

It pretends at being Thailand
but the grass is too short,
the geckos are tamed,
the chili is mild,
the fish are fed twice a day,
and the birds are on a timer.

The tide is told when to come in.

The tsunamis have a warning.

The Thais speak English.

Australians everywhere: I could be in Cairns.
Children in superman t-shirts
complaining about heat
and hiccups and mosquitos and that the pancakes
are too small.

The resort kills poems.

Waiting to be stung

The elephant has a chain
around its front left leg.

It carries its white human cargo.
It is dutifully washed.
It tries not to snatch bananas at the end.

It is made to walk
through a field full of low palms
without snaffling a single branch.

The elephant is dust
and bone and a metal seat
that it growls beneath while
our feet rest
on the top of its skull.

In a brief moment of rest
it stands beneath a rubber tree.
It stands and is glad
for the ants that jump from leaf to shoulder,
for the red sting,
for the reminder of a life that is not this.

This dust bone bleak sun scrub bake photo lake take.

For a life that is leaf stamp ant bite blade shunt hunt shade lay.
Not this. Not this.

Smother

The children do not sleep
enough. They drown
in the heat. They eat
banana cake for breakfast
and then gulp smoothies
for the rest of the day.

They miss Lego and trams,
babycinos and our tiny deaf dog.
They talk about their beds,
and Weetbix, and the cat.

They climb me constantly.
Monkeyed, I swallow fish
steamed with lemongrass
and chili. Smothered, I
look out to the hills
in my wet skin and do everything
I can to not throw them off me.

In the pool, the littlest one
floats near me (always near me), the blue
all around, and I cannot resist.

I put my foot against his back.
Sole between shoulder blades. Old
skin flattened between those small ridges of bone.

I bend my knee. I push.

I watch him float away.
And for one moment, it is only me.
The blue. The steaming water.
Sun pierced. Chili dazzled. Lemongrass steeped. Coconut baked.

Slaked.

Songkran

Songkran. Thai new year
and water is
thrown to bless
and bomb.

We stay in the resort,
worried that the children
are too small for so much
unexpected wetness.

We perform a tamer version
next to the Joy Pool. As the water
is quietly spurted
all I can feel is the urge
to chaos, is my regret at
not being out amongst it,
being bombed.

Trawling for tuna

Mr Chai's feet are flattened
and dark brown. His toes
permanently spread ready
for swell: the base of his
balance. His is a body
carved by work, and boats,
and the sea.

He carries Zach on his shoulders
to his blue and red boat. We
follow with Benji and a bag,
keeping the camera dry.

He puts his shorts back on and
stows fried rice under the seat,
watermelon in an ice-filled esky.

He lets out the lines, and we trawl.
I feel the sea in my stomach.
I watch the horizon and breathe.
Salt enters our skins.
We catch tuna, silver glitter blue gasping flipping,
that are unhooked and left to fight air
in a styrofoam box.

Benji laughs at death.
Zach slumps on the bench seat and stares.

Sal and I guard the edges,
and smile, and point to birds
and splashes: the signs of a haul.

We talk about surface and depth,
about what we can't see.
Aporiaie. Layers of lives. Lacunae.

Reaching without knowing yet what we will find.

Slicing

Knife. Mango.
No plate.
Cupping cheek.
Knife through fruit
skin and then my skin.

Knife. Flesh. Red gape.
Fruit.
Sweet. Salt. The way they go together.

He doesn't notice bloom. He wants
cheek cut into squares
that he can pull off the skin
and chew.

Orange and red drops.
A white flannel to clean
all of us. And then to hold
over the gape
while he eats.

He chews. I press.
He swallows. I press.

I throw away skin and pip.
I rinse flannel and wipe his face
and hands. Cheek from cheek.
Skin from skin. The blood does not stop.

The fruit is eaten.

Sail Rock

On the walk up to Sail
Rock, Similan Island, white beach,
postcard water, white people
posing bizarrely in the shallows
in bikinis while the ocean pushes at them;

on the walk up to Sail
Rock, a walk that three
different people say is too steep
for my three year old
son who is more nimble than
most of them with his skitter
quick feet and an eye that
catches cracks and caterpillars,
caves and chrysalis;

on the walk up to Sail
Rock, there are tree roots pushing
up through sand, tree roots
that make steps for me and
my son, that carry us to the
top to see more white people
posing bizarrely on the rocks on
the island on spread bottoms
in the sun;

on the walk up to Sail
Rock, I stub my toe against
a tree root and my son
doesn't notice and the white people
don't see and the sun keeps sunning
and I cry, and keep moving

(hobbling), and later, the next
day, know it is broken from
how bruised it is. How
swollen, how it will not
be walked on properly for weeks;

on the walk up to Sail
Rock I learn about posing, and biting
down pain, and pride in small legs
and the way wet stone feels under my feet.

On the walk up to Sail
Rock I learn about not stopping. I remind
myself that it is not important
that my children notice my tears.

Lanterns on the last night

The plan was to set lanterns
alight on the beach on
the last night
and watch them float
up like tiny suns until
we couldn't see them anymore.

But the wind was the wind.
The lanterns too thin.
The children cried and then forgot.

We packed. Went home.

Colder

Coming home Thai heat slips
from shoulders, the dead
aeroplane air leaves my lungs.
Melbourne cold licks at old
sweat. Children dance. Home.

Without Them

In the Alfama

In the Alfama everyone smokes. My
lungs, with their love of
tightening, close slightly
as soon as I walk into the air.

In the Alfama all streets are
more than cobbled, less than tiled.

In the Alfama the pasteis de nata
are always warm and doused
in cinnamon. Dogs wear bandannas
and are leadless.

In the Alfama they sing Fado all
night, and when they are finished,
have loud and heedless
conversations outside windows.

In the Alfama skylarks wheel, and
the wine and song lingers while people
smile or scowl, embrace or avoid,
put up with tourists, walk
children to school, smoke
in doorways, and remember the night.

In the Alfama they sing, every night.
Hearts are strong, from treading hills.
The streets have taught them how to love.

In the Alfama there are always cigarette butts between paving stones.
A man waits until he has passed me to spit.
On the old sandstone, graffiti that says SUZI ♡ NINES.

In the Alfama there is a woman with a knotted rope lead
wound around her chest and under her shoulder.
Next to her a tawny dog as high as my hip.
When my back is turned he jumps at me,
and I am glad of the contact from a body,
any body, that holds blood, and muscle; a beating heart.

In the Alfama I crouch in laneways to write.
No one finds this unusual.
Birds hang from washing lines in cages.
The number 28 tram, famous, dings and rattles past.
Taken over by tourists. I stay back, because I know
it is better to walk, so
poems can find me.

In the Alfama the poems find me.

In the Alfama a woman jumps in
stars to keep herself warm
while the sun drops from the sky.

In the Alfama Fado, the song of the people,
is sung by women with voices
so strong they almost break me.

In the Alfama, a globe's half turn away
from all that I know,
I am home.

On the metro

Yesterday, on the metro, I
heard an approaching accordion.
I smiled, because music on trains
does that. And when I turned
to see who was making the song,
saw a man walking down the aisle,
playing, a tiny dog on his left
shoulder, balanced neatly,
holding a small bucket
between its teeth to collect coins.

When I dropped my euros (fat coins, double rimmed) in,
I misjudged the distance, and
briefly felt the dog's gums as I
found my way to the opening. Saw pink speckled
black. Noticed the dog slightly overbalance, then correct.
The man paused while this happened, a touch, a tip,
the wet, that coining plink: their dinner.

Obrigado, said the man. The dog,
nothing.

Miradouro da Senhora do Monte

There is a fence
here that people
jump over, to drink
wine straight from the bottle.
Huddled in. One man, squatting
is picking at something green.

I want to take a picture, to catch
the moment. I imagine how I would ask
but I don't. The sun, that I have hurried
for, keeps going down. Birds make noise.
The wind against the hills like waves.

I sit, to write, and he walks past me,
between friends. Here for five
minutes. In his left hand,
what he came for:
not the view. Mint. To chop, fresh,
into potato, or to lay over grilled fish,
or ribbon onto strawberries.

The sun drops. The wind gets bigger.
The birds are birds. Over the fence
filled with locks, across the Tagus,
Jesus stands on his monolithic step (but still the smaller redeemer),
arms open, to give us his stone blessing.

The wind is the wind. The mint still grows.
Wine is still tipped, and spilt, and shared.
Here. Here is a place that knows how to sing.

Safe Haven

On the double decker bus, in the jet lag
drown, I sit on a seat with a split.
It seeps old water, and wets me without caring.

I am plugged in to a headset, listening to a recording
of a woman telling me I must try Bacalhau, salted cod.
My jeans are wet from hip to knee.
I perch weirdly on one side, hoping that the sun
and the wind will dry me.

Next she tells me the story of Fado, the song of the people,
and talks about roosters, and 550,000 people in the city,
and 3 million in Lisbon and surrounds (those seven hills).

Ulysses stopped here. And I think, what did he want?
How did he stop? What hill did his foot undo?

Jeans are still wet. I unplug. I move to a different seat.
This seat is split too. I lean again, so the water can't seep.

St. Anthony, she says, is the patron saint of Lisbon. Lost object
finder, saviour of small things. She says the word Lisbon is thought
to be Venetian: safe haven, possibly its meaning.

We finish our circuit. She starts again. I unplug.
Jeans almost dry.

Later, I try salted cod. It is fleshy, fat, tongue squint.
Later, my jeans dry.
Later, jet lag leaves.
Later, at the Feira Da Ladra, I find small lost things
to take home to my children, my lover, my friends, my sister:

    a deep tinted photo of the initiate's well in Sintra.
A plaster Mary holding her baby to be hung on a Coburg wall.
Three glazed fish and six glazed cicadas from the coast,
in blood red, and olive green, and ashen sea blue.

Later, I buy a metal rooster brightly dotted to attach to my keys,
and when I drive up Sydney Road it plickers and plings.

Safe haven. Lost things. Dry jeans.

To be kissed

A woman asks for money outside
the Pingo Dolce.

I gesture, and say,
yes, when I come out,
and she beams and puts
her palms together.

She prays.

I go in, and find coffee beans and laundry powder,
milk and a small loaf of bread,
mandarins.

I come out. I give her
my change and a mandarin and smile, and leave.

She comes after me, she grabs me from behind,
she turns me to face her, she holds me, hard.

She kisses both of my cheeks.

She smells of clothes that are old and full of outside sleep.
Her shoes are nothing. She smells of smoke and heroin and grief.

She's trying to pick my pocket, I think.
She won't let me go.

But then I know. She is still beaming into my eyes.
She still holds me. She does not break away. She will not break.

She wants to be kissed.
So I lean into her slept in clothes and cigarette breath, her chemical stain, that grief,
and I kiss her. On both of her perfect, pocked, sun stricken cheeks.
I make a loud, kissing sound, twice.
She smiles. She lets me go.

She waves. I wave. And then we walk away,
each of us carrying the smell of the other.

Still, bastard I, around the corner stop,
and check my pocket for my phone. I even
unzip my bag to catch a glimpse of my wallet that yes,
is nestling there underneath the rolls and coffee and fruit.

She wanted to be kissed.

Parque

In the pastry-laced morning I descend
and the metro is dark-tunnelling, loud-thrumming.
I descend, brave traveller, and am self-satisfied
at wayfinding in another place,
languaged out. I am on the train, smug,
because I know it is the yellow line I need,
and that then I will change to the blue line, to get to Parque.

Another station. A stop. A place to get out, so that I can move up escalators, known, and walk.

But the train pulls in and this is not a station.

Bricolaged bunker, azure, when I step out of the folding train doors
I almost fall. Into blue. I am in the bluest tunnel I have ever seen.
Tile after tile: the way grout (that sand glue mix) makes way for art.

This is not a station. It is the story of a city of conquerors. It is an acknowledgement, in tiles and gargoyles and paint, of all of the peoples the Portugese have dispossessed. It is words, it is story, it is the blueness of sky wren's egg sea glazed glass; it is the blue of an old woman's fingers just before her last crackled breath.

I stand. I stand in the tiled bunker tunnel that is a station that's not a station.
I touch the walls. I place hands on gargoyles. I soak in text through plaster
    and paint. I breathe a breath full of tears.
And then one more breath.
And then leave.

Up the escalator. I think I am done.
There could be nothing more.
Parque has done its best.
But then this. Long metal oblongs tracing the walls, with quotes,
in Portugese, back lit. So the words are absences, filled with light.
From Plato, and Lao-Tse, and Deleuze. I keep walking backwards
to try to catch meaning; the escalator pushes me up. In the end,
it doesn't matter. In the end, the words are the words, the light
is the light, the escalators will not stop.

Blue station. Gargoyle hung. Breath stealing. This is Parque.

The Initiate's Well

I write this in the deep silence of a grotto.
Water from stone drips onto this page.
The way is lit by a fat tube filled with yellow globes.

This is cavern, cave, tunnel, opening, cervix, stretch, dark, light.

Under. No out. Through. Not above. I cannot not write. I squat. Water
   drips.
I let it take pen ink and turn it to rivers that trace the poem with mineral.
This poem is damp. This poem is filled with the promise of the moon.
This poem dreams of the forest
that lies above it, always stretching its roots down to meet.

I squat and am dripped on and I write. The tunnel (opening, cervix,
   stretch)
is briefly filled
with hollering French children and
then, goes still.

I stand, to walk, notebook under arm, damp flesh. Drips from not just the
   ceiling
but the sides. Those of us who walk are blessed, light followers,
seeing through rock, tapped on the back and forehead and shoulders
by Sintra's water, that is old, and laced with the passage of novices and
   nuns.

I walk. I carry paper. I am wet. Stretch, dark, light.

And what I see is a tunnel that goes down.
What I see is the cool respite of the underground.

When I finally come to it, the end, the opening out and up to the initiate's
    well,
that is a stone tower that spirals, a curling to touch open earth,
with its star at the bottom,
I am reluctant to rise.

I regret the sun washed day. Tunnel at my back. Circle of sky above me.
Those spiralling stone walls. Tourists poking their heads through and
    snapping,
endlessly, like they might catch something that way.

I am reluctant to rise, but I do. And when I begin the walk up, and out,
I find momentum, and some
kind of errant peace with each step.

Nine flights of fifteen steps. The curve of the earth.
Scraping past tourists and moss.
The intake of breath that comes with
finding exactly what is needed:
the earth, holding me, with water and stone.

Knowing that a drip can, over time,
change iron.

Knowing that what I have touched
has touched me.

Knowing that this moment will stay.

Stretch. Dark. Light. Up. Out. But always the way back down.
Always. The Way. Back. Down.

All I Can Do

For two days I don't know what to do.
Alone, I walk.
And walk.
And walk.
The city wants feet, and breath; the steadiness of a sure tread.

It is hills and doorways, distressed paint.
It is sandstone and graffiti. It is the line of an imperfect shadow.
It is wayfinding. It is lostmaking. It is content.

In the late afternoon I find a café and sit. I order a salad
that is pear and smelly cheese and baked bread.
Lettuce, tomato, mustard seed. I eat. I drink. Content.

This city is water and brick. It won't be known.
All I can do is tickle its hide.
All I can do is walk, and sit, and eat, and drink.

All I can do is write. And hope to find my way home again.

Around Them

Separate

I was delivered by forceps. The dent
in my skull, up above my right ear,
was a party trick as a teenager,
an annoyance when I wanted to shave
my head down to the bone
at eighteen.

At thirty-four
I discovered a second dent
behind my left ear.
It had been waiting
there, that dipping, concave bone.

It had been waiting
for me to sit on the blue couch
my legs crossed, the floorboards caramel
with sun, my head tilted to rest on my left
palm. It had been waiting for my fingers to
trace it, to find its edge, to recognise its moment,
its imprint; finally, declarative, it sang.

My skull holds the footprint of those silver
clamps. My bones say here, and here, this
is where I was pulled
from you.

I have seen babies being born
this way. They don't slide out all sealish
and purple and slippy. They are pulled.
The person holding the forcep handles uses
their whole body weight to yank the
baby out. It makes me squirm, all that

pulling, those tiny neck bones concertinaing
out, the silver scoops sinking into the skull
and leaving prints, like a warm spoon
in dough.

The urgency of separation,
of the need to make two things
from one.

Rallying

At twelve I was sure. This body
would belong, even briefly, to no other.
I had watched my mother
with my sister and I, the two
children that were meant to change
her life (we changed her life),
and it did not look enticing. The days
had an edge to them, and I remember
it not like a knife, but something
blunter, something that scraped,
and was rusted, and hurt
in a slow and dull way that rarely
showed. Sometimes I wished
for blood, as if that would make it easier.
Bruised. We were all bruised.

Her voice was this beautiful thing, low
and strong but with a break. She insisted
that she couldn't sing, but she did. She sang
me into each day, and carried me through
the night. Language that tore but also
soothed, her voice, the tone of her, running
through my limbic system, coating my amygdala,
teaching my cingulate cortex about pain.

But sometimes we'd put Buddy Holly
or X-Ray Specs on the record player,
the plastic arm hooking across, the needle
coming down to rest and crackle across
vinyl, and sing, and dance on the floorboards.
Six feet banging down, chalk dust
and crayon crumbs flying up, and over it all
her reaching voice, that cracked on the no more.

It was 1979, and we were blonde girl children
with a mother who was cracking, yelling
bondage up yours and jumping off
second hand couches like we could fly.
It was 1979, and my mother was writing
for Spare Rib and wearing overalls
and gymboots and smoking rollies
and taking us to rallies.

We swam naked in the Hyde Park fountains
after Land Rights marches. Cold brown water,
one cent pieces glinting on the concrete bottom,
too far down to reach. The feel
of a metal turtle back between my five year old
legs, cool and hard and round. Balancing
on a turtle shell and dangling my legs
and looking up at the fig tree canopy, so green,
with the sun on my back, and looking over
at my sister dog paddling to the edge, her hair
gone stringy, so blonde it was almost white.

Don't think it was all bruises and cracking. There
were moments like these. There were always
moments like these: metal, and sun, and green,
and cold to the knees, and later water
and apples on the bus home,
and my mother smoking (because
you could then), and us rolling up our white and purple tickets
and pretending to do the same.

Echo

Repetition. When I take away punctuation I move to repetition.
Like this.

What is missing when I write my child
hood what I leave out is
what should come what I leave
out is what should come out from
this pen this pen writes what is missing

when I write my child
hood without punctuation I resort
to repetition which is also reiteration this
happened this
happened this
happened stop repeating yourself is what
I think because what is repetition but an echo why
do you ache towards echo

echo is the thing repeating itself in diminishing returns
echo is the moment in the dark when the walls make themselves heard
echo is the self speaking back to the self quietly without demand
i am here it says
i hear you it says
i am here

when I write my child
hood without punctuation there is room for
the darkness of cupboards and that space
under the bed
where no adult goes
where there are dust balls and Lego pieces
where I go with Big Ted taking

his yellowness with me the patch
on his back where no fur will grow because
he fell against the bar
heater and it will not grow back I do not
understand that he does not live
that no fur will grow back

I am under the bed Big Ted is under the bed we
are under the bed with dust balls and Lego pieces and
the ends of incense sticks that have burnt down to almost nothing
and then fallen and I know this is where I will
find a place to repeat

to repeat the self as if that is a meaningful thing
to imagine I am out under a sky that presses down on my skin
to shout words from lungs warmed by blood and the song of the
    afternoon
to dream of a time when I will see my own face in the mirror and it will
    not be this

this childling who owns nothing and takes refuge in bedroom caves with
    bears

under the bed I go under the bed and I know I am home.

Knowings

It is not that there is nothing left.
It is not that the snow bites
and takes all life as it lays itself down.

There is stone here, the icy
breath of earth. Roots, branches
that point blackly and say

here. It was here that the flames
came down, as if they had never
known restraint.

It is through this that we walk.
Tracing old paths. Noticing earth, stone, branches,
roots; the way that fire and snow make themselves known.

Salt remembers

When I write about desire I almost can't put
my finger on it, that slipping place
an arc of wetness, pearling, the way I always grapple
with blood.

When I write about desire I end up tied down,
I end up wrapped around
you I end up aching to be crushed like
salt rocks dropped to the floor and turned to grit
under your heel like being pushed under the
surface like the floor is a horizon like we are moving
into sunbright sky like blue is more than a colour
like blue is more than this day that wraps itself
around the both of us and gathers my voice with its
moan and laces the lilac tree with it. Because sound travels
and the window at the front of our house always
wants to hear more.

When I write about desire my fingers remember
all the places they have been, and begin to curl,
cupping every warmth they have ever held
in the centre of a mnemonic fist. As if my hand were
an embryo. As if the anatomy of my hand cradled every
moment and had never forgotten how to hold it, still.
Still. In the night, against the sheets, it will grab
at everything it can find. It will say this, and there,
this is how I know you, this is what I knew then. It will
ask for more, it will say this is almost never enough. You will
tell me (again) how greedy I am. And my body will remember.

The body will remember. Later, it will tell the story of the night,
the afternoon, the darkling day. Later, it will dream red, and electric,
and shooting, and blunt. Later, it will ache after sensation like salvation.

Later, it will tell you desire is what makes us who we are.

It will ask you why you insist
on not-remembering this. It will draw a line
you have never seen before: it will show you
where flesh meets, where it stretches and beats.
It will describe for you an edge that has lost its edge.

It will say here, here,
this is where you touch me.

Here.

Later, it will make a nest for you. It will curl you into itself.

It will tell you a story. It will talk to you
about its beating heart, the crushed salt, its fist.

It will tell you that blue is more than a colour, that the window
is a mirror that draws pictures with your moans.

It will remind you that the floor is a horizon.

That we are all grains beneath feet.

That we are all fists, closing around memory, looking for bliss.

The body is salt.
The body is water.
The body is ocean, waiting to escape.

Absorption

My outsides gather rain
from the air. I cycle through.
My outsides gather wetness
from the air as I pass.
My outsides draw water through
the barrier of my skin because it is not
a barrier. Because it is full
of holes. Because this is the very definition
of porousness. My outsides
gather rain from the air.

The layer underneath my skin
is desperate for the wetness of the day.
Dry too long, it wants a damp
salvation.

How are you dry? They ask this, when I pass.
You are all fat and blood and tissue.
You are already mostly water.

They will never know all
of the ways I am dried and desiccated;
how paper lives underneath my skin;
how bark has taken the place of organs;
how rough the core of my abdomen is;
how there is sandpaper between my thighs;
that my heart is a balloon filled with sand.

When it squeezes, it bulges
like a soft ball held too hard.
It protrudes top and bottom; you can see
the outlines of grit.

My outsides are desperate
to drink the day. Absorption
is the method. Wetness,
the outcome, but like desire,
it will be fleeting, and unsatisfied,
and after the peddles have stopped peddling,
and I am
        inside
out of the rain, I will always
be dry again. The sand will win. I will be
a bag of grain. I will seek damp. I will try
to lick it from the insides of your cheeks the next time we meet.

You will not understand, and find me too needy. We
will turn from each other. One dry, one wet. Nothing damp. No leaks.

Ash and breath

When I wake, my asthma is not
as bad as the day before. Relief from
the catch and grip, respite, whole breaths
that go unnoticed. We are in
Newcastle and there is tea in an old
friend's house, who has hair so white
it is sand or clouds or cotton wool and
the tea is earl grey and the milk
is full cream and we sip, and talk, and
rest our feet on empty chairs, and she
waves her cigarette smoke away from me.

Is that when it starts? Catch and grip.
Noticing breath.

I go quietly to the room that holds my backpack
and find spacer, find puffer, perform the ritual of fours.
I return to tea and more talking. It is thirty-two degrees.
The wind runs at us, at the lemon tree. The dog is
unsure what to chase.

Bushfire weather, we say.

The day moves into itself, the talking resolves. We
show each other photographs of our children, and old
friends, as if this will replace the decade that stands between us.

When it is time to go, we embrace. We hold our bodies against each other
and press into the line they make. We send love. We say see you
at Christmas, and we have missed you, and this was so lovely, and ...
In the car, on the way to the airport, the catch and grip
turns to tight and grab. More Ventolin, the ritual of fours, again.

We spend a fine hour in the cool, filtered air.
My chest settles. We drink coffee and talk about poetry
prizes, about judges, about anything but leavings, and breath.

On the tarmac we wait, and it takes time before we notice this:
fire. The smoke filled sky. Five helicopters hovering,
steel cables unreeled from their bellies, aiming conefulls
of water at the trees. That's why, I say. It's the smoke—the
air is full of smoke. I try not to think about particles, my
inflamed lungs. What is landing in me. I urge the line forward.
I need to get up those metal steps, into the body
of the bird, away from the hateful sky.

And what I want to know is, when we get up there,
what we will find? How many ways can we say goodbye?

The plane taxis, then lets itself go. Sarah Blasko sings
'Flame Trees' over the PA without irony. From my window,
as we tilt at the sky, I see this: the raging horizon,
the way smoke likes to rise in lines, what the colour
orange looks like when it carries renewal and death.

We turn left, we aim along the coast. We leave the roiling
line of bush to find its own way back into the dirt. And then
I see this: the ocean, finally, has met the sky. There is no line,
just a seamless transition. There is haze, there is the picture
of breath. We keep going up. We go into, and then over
the clouds. Sarah has stopped singing, the flame trees
blind no one. My lungs want cooling, want mist.

My lungs want a last goodbye. They want
songs that scour the ash from them,
they want unconstrained breath. They
want to stop thinking, always,
about ins and outs. They dream,
loudly, of strength. And often,
of rest.

Reverberation

They X-ray my lungs as if looking through
me will tell them something: as if
those graining grey pictures will help.

Do you have any metal on? Yes. I
have nipple rings, I say. There is
always silence when I say this. Always because
my lungs have been looked at more than
once. Because when I go to hospital they like to press me
against a lined plate, shivering, breath held, to hunt down
shadows and crushed glass; to capture the crackle and wheeze.

They know these rings are not for them.

Silver looping through flesh, a gasp, a screaming breath.

In hospitals, steel and desire do not mix.
In hospitals, steel is for cannulas and speculums, for cracking
chests, for the legs of whining beds.

Yes, I have nipple rings, I say. And there it is: the absence
of noise that is not silence, that comes after speaking, out
of place.

It is what is left after the shot has rung out
it is everything drilled down to quiet in the aftermath
it is the tinnitus ring, the screaming din. It is the sound
of death, reverberating.

The X-ray is done. Shiver and breath. Later mist, and blood
pressure cuff, and the way hospital gowns unwrap me, the way they
    conspire

to show more than they cover. The obscene white and blue. The incessant beeping. The groans from the next bed, because there are always groans from the next bed.

In between, nothing.

The early morning hours roll out from under me.

Water gathers, unheard, underneath my silver plated ring.

When I take it off the next day it has left a red and blistered band around my right index finger.

I have been scalded by love, by jewellery, by the meeting point of trapped fluid, and skin.

Two days later, on the train, I notice the blister
has dried and I can't help but pick at it. Peel it. Pull it away.

Coruscating, the skin flakes fall to the glittering ground. The people around me
tap at their phones and carefully pretend my cells are not travelling, drily, to meet them.

Necrosis

Dragonfruited sphere,
shining tissue,
black spotted ball,
bloodless moon.

You are nestled in bowel.
You are torsing. You double me
over. You double what I see:

the folded blanket that rucks
nastily behind the back
behind the back of my head,
the wall spouting tubes,
a chair prickling out from the corner;
whiteness glaring at whiteness.

They have run out of pillows.
He (the doctor, the one with the wand) can't find you.

You bloom, necrotic, spotted, carrioned.
Dead egg carrier you torse, you double, you
shout at the tear that is my
groin back ribs leg knee throat back
back back back back.

He can't find you. They talk
about us in the third person not knowing
we are fourth person poetic split by pain.
They want to send us home.

Dragonfruit: bloom, split, tear, twist, turn.
But they do. Find you. They spear
you and bag you. Pull you through
a hole in my belly after their metal scissors
snip at your stalk. Dead moon. Distended.

And then.

And then you are gone.

You are gone already and I have never seen you.
You were mine. You were opening and closing,
globing, the light that is thrown by belly dreams
and babies.

And when I wake, with a drain and a drip
and a pillow and a morphine button
to press, you are gone.

You are black tissue in a bag.
You are hazard, removed, and the absence of pain.
Ovary. Egg layer. Possibility thrower.

Gone.

Proof

Morphine poems
are bright, jittering things. Glimmer
glitter in the night gut red,
slickly bright.

They follow
the judder of the building
and scribe earthquakes, dust,
that shaking moment where
everything is
turned to nothing, brightly, with
chaos.

Morphine poems have castles
in them; shards of quartz that fly.
They are beaming moments they
follow lines of flight they make me
feel brilliant and shimmery
in the night.

There is a moment,
drowning in a nest of hospital cotton,
the pump dinging, prongs that shoot
oxygen into my nostrils, pain,
webbing drug, there is a moment
when I am streaming into light and
quartz castle
the earthquake all around.

There is a moment
where I am no ordinary poet,
and the stitches in my belly, the hole
where my uterus used to be, are the proof.
No ordinary poet, me.

Morphine dream stream shining
firebright gold shooting out doubling
in. There is a moment when it is all worth this
moment, here.

This morphine dream.

Outline

In the afternoon I decide to walk. My clothes
are wrong and so are my shoes. I have just come
from a day of work; I smell of classrooms. I am imbibed
with whiteboard marker, my hands are blue and red from
being used as rubbers. My feet are empty—they have been
standing for too long. In the staffroom they rested, but wanted
more. So in the afternoon I decide to walk.

There is a track. It traces the Mitchell River. I walk. I see seven
different kinds of birds in the first fifty metres. It would be
more poetic if I could name them all (my grandmother could
name them all). As it is, I take note of elongated beaks, outstretched
wings, wet feathers, outstretching webbed feet, streaks of colour
against the eye; a certain sleekness tracing its way across the water.

There is a track. The sun is moving downwards, withdrawing its heat,
giving it away somewhere else. In the last of its light it gives
shadows to the pebbles underneath my boots: it gives the gift
of doubling, and when I bring my eye down, every stone
has a dark doppleganger. Every stone knows both itself and its other.
    Every
stone aches to be trodden on, if only to shift, to throw a new shadow,
to reconsider its place on the track; to be something else in this moment
of light and shade, with the sound of a human moving past.

I have direction. I tread on doubled stones. The wet birds stay wet. The
sun keeps moving down, taking itself away.

I walk and as I walk I let myself go. Every piece of the day
(my red and blue hands, the muttering of adolescents, squashed
grapes in the hall, a fifteen year old almost, but not quite, crying
in an office with hard carpet and harder walls)

lays itself down amongst the shadows and their stones. Every piece
of the day sighs, and lets me go. I walk, I walk, I walk.

I notice the breath of bugs against my skin. Cooler air. A change in the
    way
I move. Light. Shift. A settling into evening. The blessing of twilight.

I walk and I find the tops of trees. The sky coming down to meet them.

I see that what matters is the outline of things against the sky
the way that outline draws the eye
down to trace bracken or leaf loss, those mourning cockatoos.

Beside the track are berries so purple they sing. Globing
from stalks. Shaking brightly at me. Waiting to be
threshed between teeth. That beguiling squirt before
the poison hits. The adolescent sheds her tears. The cockatoos
grieve. The berries wait, to shake themselves at the next walker.
The stones have their shadows stolen by the night. No sound.
No human goes here.

Gingerly

rhizome you unbind me
        I am reach and unknown and ache
I am a thousand trembling plateaus that speak to a thousand more
        I am you

I am not root I am not tree I am not leaf not bark not sap not sun in the green
        I am underground writhing turning away from light
wormsearching, heartlurking, catching words to feel their ginger spike
        against tongue
    and throat,
against voice
    and hope.

                Be quick, they say. Run, don't plant. Offshoot.

        Shooting off I write silverfast I grab at text as it
burrows
    shivers
        connects.

        I grab at text like it is making meaning where I lie. Like it will still be
here
later. When I leave. When every part of me is dustmaker and you can't
            remember the colour of my eyes
    the way I sound when I cough. That stretch. I grab. At text.

Coming and Going

The thing is I had never seen death up so close.
On the plane I held the breadwarm body of my baby
and tried to see the ground.

I hoped you would wait for us, for him.

What did I know about you? What would I lose
when you were gone? A God Bless on the phone
two or three times a year. The memory of finding
you, the sound of your voice recognising mine.
A grandmother I had known by name
become real. Somerset accent,
a fine gold cross around your neck ready
to be clutched, a poodle
that guarded you from table tops.

We landed. I found my sister by the baggage carousel,
was glad for her glossy lips, the diamantes in the arms
of her glasses, her shine against my Melbourne black.
We drove Canberra's wide roads and she
said 'Granny's very poorly', and 'it might be a shock'.

My baby grabbed at sunlight while I tried
to make myself ready.

But the thing is I had never seen death
up so close so I wasn't. Ready.

For the greyness of your skin.
The cavern of your mouth.
Your gusting stale breaths.

They said your bones were breaking
as you lay. They had not given you food
or drink for days. I sat and held your hand,
your large boned brittle fingers twitched.

I held my baby close and introduced you. I put his hand
in yours and saw his hermit crab fingers scrabbling over your palm.

One arriving, one leaving.

You moaned, then sighed with your heaving
and rattling chest. He wriggled and kicked.

It would be days yet, but we could not stay.
Back on the plane I could still smell old
saliva and saline. Back on the plane my baby
sucked, and held my thumb in his fist, and slept.

Autocorrect is becoming a scourge

I find out you will be gone by Winter
five minutes before work begins.
'I have bad news, do you want it now, or later?'
Rachael asks.
      On the walk to work I was wrapped around by a headache:
the fierce headphones next to me on the train
the spat with Sal before leaving
Benji saying over and over 'I want to go *hoooome*'
in the hope that enough repetition would
      force capitulation, would make all of us bend
      to his four year old will.
'Now,' I say because it is better to learn things quickly,
then take those learnings away, to enfold, to pull into the depths
of the belly, the spine, the throat, later, alone.
      On the walk to work, before I know anything except
      headache that moves into my jaw and lives there
      waiting for me to unclench,
      a child praying for floorboards coated in redyellow rugs
      bodies under bedspreads, puppy nips,
      cup after cup of cold water with ice,
      a plate of salami and black olives for lunch;
      on the walk to work I see a curl of iron,
      brown leaves raked early from the NGV fountain –
      (water pretending to be untouched),
      a pregnant woman in a tight grey dress,
      material creased, her back-filled walk.
'It's Kate,' she says. 'She has bowel cancer. When they opened
her up in surgery she was riddled with it. They did a bypass
to help the pain but she has weeks, maybe
months, to live.'

And then we have to work. We are both interpreters.
We interpret a research methods class. We take turns.
It is my go first. The lecturer talks about word
counts and gives examples of H1 projects
and rocks back and forth on his heels
and taps his whiteboard marker and I sign what he says
because that's my job but all I can think is
       I haven't seen you for at least a year. I still
       have your tureen. The cream one with flowers
       and fussy handles. You brought it to my house
       one day, filled with cous cous and almonds. I tried
       to organise to drop it back to you but you told me not
       to worry, that I could give it to you next
       time we saw each other. But we didn't. See each other.
       And now you are in hospital, your cells
       beating you (again).
Your cells beating you, again. As if you hadn't already had
your fair share. I waited days before I sent my first message.
I imagined you were inundated, and probably sick
of telling the story of your going. I waited, and then sent
you a poem. I don't need you to reply, I said, but you did.
I will send you poems, I said. So I did. The last thing I sent,
an essay from Oliver Sacks, dying too, cells grabbing
at him like they were at you, an essay on the renewal that
comes from being alive an extra day.
You loved it. You sent me a drug addled message
about good hears and I/U (hearts, I thought,
something about the two of us and hearts).

I meant to reply. In the shower this morning, the water
hot, steam on the shower screen showing an old drawing
of Benji's: bulbous body, stick legs, cavernous mouth,
pinprick eyes, I composed a reply.

But when I got out, a red towel, fresh, around me, shower
steam following me from the bathroom, a ghosting trail,
Rachael had called me. I knew.

I knew as soon as I saw it. I got dressed. I made tea,
and sourdough toast. I patted the puppy. No.

She called again. I answered. I answered and I knew. And she
knew I knew. But she told me anyway.

The sky is full of clouds and ravens yell while the rain
starts coming down. I put the rubbish out. The ants
busy themselves getting out of the pelt. I am careful
not to let the puppy slippery slink
past me fast out to the street where he will
not come when I call no matter what the prize I hold.
I move, slow with the fact of your going,
in the rain, to the back yard. There are towels
on the line. Four of them. Two big, two small. Still dry.
Clothes line on my right
    I meant to visit you last week
Trampoline on my left, always waiting to be jumped on
  I meant to reply to your text message last night
Raspberry bushes behind the trampoline, rain.
   You wrote to me about your last addled message
I see some of them are ready, are waiting to be taken
   that autocorrect was getting the better of you

I stand, in the rain, and coax them bloodily into my hands
        so much pain, too many drugs, you laughed even then
the trick not to pick, but to let the globing clusters come to rest
        ha ha, you wrote, I meant to say you have a good heart
in the palm. Picking squashes and separates, leaves us with nothing.
        I meant to say thank you for sending me that poem
        I loved it and will think more about it later,
        it's so complex

I meant to say bloody autocorrect. It gets the better of me on a good day
and here is another poem for you to read because
I sent them to you, on and off, when I knew you were going.

When I visited you in the palliative care ward we talked
about which ones you wanted at your funeral.
'You know what I like' you said. I don't.
I don't know. I kept hoping you would be decisive,
would say I want Audre Lorde and Maya Angelou,
that'll do. These two, from this collection. But you didn't.
You kept leaving it to me.

In front of your son you gave me the name of the song
you wanted played, told me I'd know it. You'll never
be the sun by Dolores Keane. I nodded, wrote it down.

And today when Rachael told me you were gone I couldn't find
it, the paper with your writing, the name of the song. I
upended my little green bag full of chewing gum wrappers
and pens, my notebook, a small tube of sun cream
for the kids. Frantic. Refusing that it might be gone.

I looked until it was found,
in a tiny tucked away pocket,
nestled between business cards and
a blood test form.

When I visited you in the palliative care ward you
asked for vanilla chai and when I
brought it back the foam laced your half dropped
mouth. The surgery from years ago
that took a tumour from your hearing nerve had
severed the muscles that kept that side of your face
up, and now it was hard to drink. You sipped
from a straw.

'I just can't believe it,' you said in your too loud
voice (deaf from that first surgery, volume was
no easy thing) 'three weeks ago I was about to start
a new job, and now here I am, and there's
not enough time. I wanted to say goodbye
to everyone slowly, but there's so many of you, and
it's going so fast.' You laughed. You were conspiratorial
as you sipped your forbidden chai.

But today you are gone. And I don't know
what poems to put in your funeral booklet.
And I still have your tureen.
And my hands are stained with raspberry blood,
and the air carries rain.

You told me once that what you missed most
after that surgery, the one that made you deaf,
that bought you a language you could speak with your body,

was the sound of rain on a tin roof. The loudness of it.
The way it wouldn't be described. That if you
could not sleep, this was the sound
you tried to conjure.

Today you are gone and it is raining. The raspberries
I picked are sitting on the dark wooden bench
in a small glass bowl. I will find you
your poems.

Coalesce

~~I am already dead.~~ Already, I am dead.
~~I am gone.~~ Already, I am gone.
You are reading this when I am gone.

Dis. Integrate.

Already I am earth   ash   leaf   caterpillar,
the tomato between your teeth.

Already I am ink on the page the bottom
of your boot tepid water from a sun
soaked tap, wood.

Dis. Integrate.

Already I am dust mote that cannot fit
inside itself, small parts flung out and
around and under, blood shiver, glass shard,
prism throwing light at the yellow kitchen walls.

Already I am dug down with a sign skewered
above me in the soft dirt my children dug out
earlier: this is the grave where I lay, where
I lie, where I am folded inside a pillow case.

I am my own terrier tucked in, dead from
the green syringe the vet brought to our house
at eleven am. My arm shaved.
Anaesthetic put in. I am the dream of dirt
and bone. I am put down. I am put under.
I am touching root systems, gravel, earthworm.
I am carried by me and my three year old

who cradles my head while I take
the weight of my body.
My eyes refuse to close.
My tongue keeps pushing out
between the loose points of my teeth.

Dis. Integrate.

~~I am gone.~~ Already, I am gone.

Digging

I am not the poet. It's not
me you're thinking of. I do not
sigh. I do not lie on grass
crinkling under me
and notice the gleam
on fig leaves leaving.

I am not the poet. It's not
me you saw with patches
on my elbows eyeing
off salamander eggs and
caribou steaks. I will not
be fed wine, drip by aching
drip, by some patron
somewhere long ago.

I am not the poet. No
laudanum laces my veins. I
have no questions about beauty, or
truth, or the porcelain
state that is lives
linked together by love.

I am not the poet. Long
afternoons interrupted
by cheese and moving
the rug to catch the last
of the sun are not for me.

All I can do is drill down
to the detail in one swift
moment, in between

my children thinking I
am climbing pole, question
answerer, food provider, love
giver.

All I can do is notice
the way a steel fence holds
me out, the way warning
signs say more about who
wrote them than what they caution
against, how construction
machines, still in the growing
morning, look as if they have
been digging all night, on
a secret project
of their own, and fallen
into slumber where they stand,
and in that sleep dream of dirt,
and what lies beneath,
and the way that digging
down teaches us about
depth, and what lays
hidden, and foundations,
and the softhard cradle of the
earth as it embraces the yellow
teeth of machines,
searching after dark, trying
to make up for all of that shooting
buildings into the sky
day after day.

The salamander eggs are
cracked and shimmering.
The caribou steaks lust
for the body of the beast
they were sliced from.

I am not the poet. I.

What Comes Next

Glisten

That glaze, the way it drips
and licks at mousse and sponge;
no room for air, gold laced,
aching onto the plate.
You break into it, silver tines
turned to spears, chocolate as dark
as the night, catching at the corners
of your mouth, sugar laced,
smoother than skin. Spear, eat,
glistening bliss. We kiss.

Fruitpicker

Untangle, turn. Blackberry vines twitch.
Smell of blood, salted moon.
Stained.
Juice mapped, Queensland on this stomach.
Your last rib.
Allusion.
I am Eve.

This is not style. I am hazed by the bubbling slip,
saliva of word on paper.

You swallow sugar cubes whole.
Syrup murmurs glaze my tongue.

Do I tell you of parchment thin skin?
Fiction and firelight?
When I flew your last gift to the sea, I could not
spy silver through the waves.

You read religion in thorn and leaf. Crown and cloth.
Soil pimples my thigh and the grate of berry seeds
between teeth louder than anything.

I pluck you from me.
Bats sing.

Flour

You smother me with
your featherlight kiss,
your creamy skin.
Flick away,
skip slow. I tread
my weight to the board,
trailing the angel dust of your joints.
Your smile dusky,
cochineal lips lift my skin away,
careful as cooked meat from the bone.
You dance and grin delicious.
I am ready.

Radiation

I have not met
you yet. We left I
was four and in the stories
you
were a madman.
Violent. Locking me
in cupboards. Washing
evil spirits from my mother's shoes
at 3am. She found you
there on the shower floor with her pink
gym boots and her ugg boots and
thongs scrubbing at the soles
to fix everything. In the stories you
believed in aliens, the Age
of Aquarius. That dragons ruled. You sat
opposite the TAB and
used numerology and odd
charts to predict
the next
win.

But today
you emailed me after 29 years
and said 'I still use some
of your baby language—sultanas
were "tahnles" and you were very
fond of saying "sucking itchles" when
you itched.' And suddenly I
knew you had known
me
had heard me
speak before

we left. Before
I was four.

And then in the next email you said
you
were worried
about radiation. It went
for two pages that I should
drink
pineapple juice to counteract all
of that radiation in
the air, the food,
the secret radar
weapons, the microwaves.
And I felt it grip
in me
the old wariness the reason
I want to keep you
at
arms
length.
All that radiation.

The Second Cup

At the first hot sip, I know
it will not do. Not
milky enough, its colour too deep.
I wait until you leave
the room and then
sneak, half defiant and half
ashamed, to our buttery kitchen.
I hope you will not hear me tip
your work away to make room
for the water poured hot, the three minute
steep, the finger width of milk.
You are coming down the hall
as I tread back, carrying the perfect drop.
I can only pretend that none of this
has happened and take my place
on the new brown couch.
I sit. I sip. I sip.

Toe glue (tell)

Kahlo put her toes back on with painter's glue.
I imagine bristles pulling from her brush and
getting stuck between foot end and
gangrenous digit.

Glue—
Toe.
Azure stain from another self portrait,
from shawl laced with skin cells and laudanum, from peacock feather dulled,
from bird speaking to paint to pain to paint.

Pain t   pain   t   pain   t   pain   t.

Later the bristles will stick into her between
shoe leather and black nail.
Yellow, the bristle. Brown, the leather.
Black, the nail.

In a room. All those implements. What will she
use to paint with? Is there a brush with more
bristles balanced on the bed head that may be she
can reach?

Pain t. Pain t. Pain t. Pain ( )
       ( )   toe
       ( )   bristle
       ( )   empty brush
       ( )   azure
       ( )   birds egg dead crack
       ( )   glue
       ( )   leather constrain constraint the pain t. Take.

Swim

Water holds memory
it knows its way back.
Clouds grey white the roiling
sky a storm promising presence and absence both.

Sand here is coarse it scrubs
our feet we drop clothes
into a pile, skewer water
bottle, and walk to salt
beat the heat binders
gone breath unconstrict.

I squeal you plunge.

Melbourne boy made soft
by heated pools and the
oceanless Northern suburbs
where I find respite at the creek.
You plunge and butterfly
out ahead the brown of
your back a fleshy turtle
shell. Your arms pointing
the way to horizon, to home.

You come up grinning
you tell me to go all the
way
in.

On the next wave
I dive strive the salt
hitting eyes I come up
you are there.

We are push pulled
in the chop we are gaze.
Water swallowed
ocean cooked sky licked
we are octopus arms
slippery legs strong bellies
a flicker flash of
this.

      You fit. You just fucking fit,
you say in your tear strung voice on the phone, in bed,
over water, under cover.

You're for me, I say throwing
fear, knowing rightness,
feeling sure like roots in soil: vine climbing, branch reaching, shoot
seeking.

The storm does not come. It
stays half the sky. We
swim and dive, we shoulder
ride. We shoulder ride!
You go down I slip my
feet around your back
lace my hands to settle them
on the top of your head.
You push up, you brace.

I am big this is no whippet
thin circus trick this is pure
strength. Your chin just out
of water you face the waves.
We laugh like we have beaten gravity. I lose balance. We
both fall, and come up
spitting the almost storm, laughing more.

Looking up there is cloud and not,
the yellow light of rain wanting to come,
the cold whip of wind bringing wet.
We swim, drift, laugh, hold, kiss.

Lips touch lips, hands hips, toes find calves,
eyes find what comes next.
What comes next?

Where I Write

The yellow kitchen table. Laminate, sixties echoing off the top, bits of Weetbix that won't come off, no matter what I do.

The shadows of callistemons. These are the trees that drop thin leaves all year, that call the birds in, that wash away the city air, that threaten to fall.

The big window. It lets the shadows in and on its sill sit a red buddha, a sculpture from a friend that's a ball of pins, two white and blue egg cups, and a glass jug full of wooden spoons and tongs.

Under my feet are slate grey tiles: too cold in winter even with socks and slippers on. In summer they get warmer as the day goes, and by 5 o'clock I can't remember them ever being cool.

On the bench to my left sits the kettle with its silver hide. It will boil me through the day. It will make more cups of tea than it wants to. It bubbles and clicks, and hopes for rest. On the bench to my left sits the butter dish, that will hand over globes of fat to be spread over toast, its thick ceramic walls fending off the flies that like to find their way around the screen door's edge.

This house was built by a man who worked at the Princess Theatre on Spring Street. While he was there they pulled up the floor, and he took three planks of the thickest wood I have ever seen home with him. He turned the planks into the bench that holds the kettle and butter dish. This is the bench I chop vegetables on. This is the bench where grapefruits bleed and onions leak. This is the bench that holds up school lunches and biscuit crumbs, that knows the feeling of small hands scrabbling over its top and dreams of dancing feet and a timpanic shake.

This is where I write. At the yellow kitchen table, in the shadows of callistemons. I alternate mouthfuls of tea with vegemite toast. I notice the colour of wood.

The theatre floorboards throw their history at me. Music plays. The children are gone. The cat has been fed. And all I am is table, and tea, and keyboard, and shadows, and toast: all I am is a catchment for dancing feet and the memory of theatre. This is where I write.

Tender Bodies

This is a re/production of Gertrude Stein's 1914 prose poem *Tender Buttons (Objects • Food • Rooms)*. All text in italics is lifted/loved/taken from that text.

BOYCUNT
The difference is spreading.

WHAT IS IT

People want to know at dinner but suppose dinner is a house and the work is never done and no one will eat the rainbow shards thrown by crystals hanging in the floor. Suppose the floor is a rubbery hollow. Suppose you have made yourself a hole that is not a hole that wants to be empty and full and eaten and revered. Suppose you are that hole.

Does this change. Does everything change. Are the children ok. Testosterone makes the sky red you will be sexually aggressive with that in you. I have that in me and crying is easier than even before but laughing is easier too. The cup is a habitus and carries me everywhere. I think about what is the opposite of a vessel. I think about how to make while I change. Are the children ok. Does this change.

The question does not come before there is a quotation. There is no question but there is every question and there is music and a loitering moon and legs that shiver when they should be still in the night in the night in the bed going down under the horizon like a brightness that should be open open open. Are you open.

I am reckless I take the yoke of an egg and swallow it whole I eat the sun *be reckless be reckless* be more be less be be be uneaten supposing you are uneaten and this is nothing at all.

It is not even more hurt than that, it has a little top. When they took my uterus and cervix they said I'd have a bucket and a blunt end and I do but now that means something but not blunt I have a sharp an eaten. Do you want more.

There is marking to be done make sure your proofread this is an admirable effort I can see you've worked hard I write all these things but *out of an eye comes research* and my research says I have a boycunt that can't be pinned down but can be open open open like I am taking all of you inside me and fucking you just.

Supposing ... supposing that there was no astonishment and no one was terrified of boxes on a form of Ms and Fs and what. How to put someone. One person. On paper how to put me there where they want me. But you had babies. But you have breasts. But you but you but what is there to say any more than a cup and a garden made from cuttings given to me on a Saturday afternoon. *A sac a small sac and an established colour and cunning* and the dirt that I thought was dead but then we found worms. So many tiny chili plants you love chili you will pick them after they have grown and a way of drawing Bromeliads to me as if Bromeliad and boycunt had found some way of touching of being near. That they should be near and people and friends knew and that is what they brought with them.

Bought or brought you ask.

My sore teeth.

LIGHT

I walk into men's toilets after taking breaths down after holding and holding the best ones are the ones that don't have urinals to walk past. All that silver. The smell. Then *to have corners, to be lighter than some weight* to draw myself on a napkin and that torn nothing paper becomes a map that changes without distress because the map changes to meet us in the late afternoon with the birds who come for the Grevillea in my new in this new in a place with rotting weather boards why is the weather in the board who knows about glass where is there light.

I send you the definition of habitus in a text message.

There is a cut on my back and *nothing breaking the losing of no little piece.*

A lamp is not the only sign of glass but when I sign it changes every thing. This is my name this is this is this is my name.

WIND

Suppose I send you the meaning of habitus and *suppose the rest of the message is mixed with a very long slender needle.* Suppose you are more than this. *What is this current. What is the wind, what is it.* On that Saturday making the garden with worms and Bromeliads there was no wind and we tore up cardboard the boxes unbecoming and made a suffocating bed for all that grass but in the morning *what is the wind* the wind was there and the cardboard was not and the boxes wanted to make themselves back.

Later I found box fragments from my garden my torn garden two or three streets away away so I could *practice the sign* and say *it is a spectacle, it is a binding accident.* Supposing I just bound and bound my chest was a boy with breasts and there were no implications.

CARELESS WATER.

It does, it does change in more water. After the wind always the rain. What is the rain, what is it. It goes deep in its itness it goes down and deep and is on skin and cement and dirt and steel and plastic and that guttered needle that still holds blood on its insides.

The sudden spoon is the wound in the decision. The decision is the sudden wound as if I couldn't see my self coming as if the others needed to be forewarned and then nursed through their shock. As if shock is a stick pushed sharply against an eyeball that gives every thing a way.

This shift from one to not quite an other is a continuing separation but in the academy where I re/produce words and works and marks and comments there is *a pleasant simple habitual and tyrannical and authorised and educated and resumed and articulate separation.* In the academy they let me change my name and I go to the men's toilet and only once or twice is it odd but never do I feel not safe. After a while in the academy I stop needing to say so much my name and all those walls but supposing there were more to say about doorways.

WRITING

THE BOOK

Is *a winning of all the blessings* and on the yellow kitchen table it continues being written but nobody knows this and they ask for spoons full of honey and the honey licks the wound and makes a yellow sheen over the blood and turns an orange tinge and I like the wound we lick *a collapse and a sold hole* and I know this hole. Supposing the hole is every thing.

THE WINDOW

You push my legs up over my head you push. You make pictures of me when I can't see. You show me later in the broken light and we kiss and the water on the window is the spit you leave on my cheeks you push you push you push.

THE LAMP

Supposing I was comatose what then. Are the children are the children they need so much and so they don't get enough. And so. And *so clean is a light that nearly all of it shows pearls and little ways* and I buy paper stars filled with light and string them across the window of my children as if to light the way.

Come and say what prints all day. What prints are these walls these words your finger prints blood up my spine a spine that crackles in your wake and shudder shivers later to the tune of a dog and a broken washing line and the hum of dirt. *This is not true.*

Count, count more so that thicker and thicker is leaning. Count the way you smell in the corridor of a chapter that is waiting for you later much later and this is knowing all the great moments and all the nothing moments supposing this is nothing. No thing.

SUPPOSE AN EYES.

Chest not valuable, be papered. Be papered and bound but the binder is tearing is not fit to wear doesn't hold anything down and the smell of rain and dirt and old citrus fills whatever room this is is there room is there what we know to be space in this room suppose I see you in the dark making pictures what then.

In feeling I know there are no questions and the day goes and music is in my bones and my bones are a white hot breakfast for the cat who has been waiting for a long time along with the children and the dog and the Bromeliads to be fed in the feeding they will learn in the feeling they will know how to be unfull much much later are the children ok. *In feeling anything is resting, in feeling anything is mounting* in feeling we find a bitten moment and pack it carefully away to be broken open later.

LOVE

When we find each the other there is an understanding that *inside the between that is turning* there are the both of us. There is recognition supposing that any heart can recognise an other there is known and knowing the children may be ok this may not be saying too much too much is not this silver beat in between where we meet. Where we meet.

The kindly way to feel separating is to have a space between and in that space between the glint of steel of a tooth of the lamp that sees what we do and the *darkness very dark darkness is sectional* and in excess of what is needed supposing anything is needed

quite

like

this

fist that finds a tunnel that holds a core that turns me open open open.

Take no remedy lightly, take no urging intently, take no separation leniently take the remedy surreptitiously before they see. We see because there is a cup and *all goods are stolen* (all text is stolen—reproduction is thievery of the most bitter beautiful kind), and *all the blisters are in the cup.*

This is today.

There is a cut along the bottom of the small of my back it is a drawing in red it is a long horizontal line that's life you said it is two cuts crossing that line that is me and that is you you said. *What is cut. What is cut by it. What is cut by it in.*

Where the first and the second small lines cross the big long line there is what could be a hole or a crossroads what is this cross where two roads meet. What is this hole how are two lines meeting and crossing whole. *A whole is inside a part, a part does go away, a hole is a red leaf.* My boycunt is a red leaf and we fuck it together because suppose *the instance of there being more is an instance of more.* And all that was required in the end was more red leaf more shine more loitering moon more supposing more writing on walls down legs in steam in the night on the arm of the one who loves and is loved in the flesh of a mango bruised from a fall under fluorescent lights in the putrid corner in the day that turns night into a threshold that turns and makes way for legs and breath. Supposing that's what this is. *Explaining darkening and expecting relating is all of a piece.*

This was thought.

A shine is that which when covered changes permission.

Almost very likely there is no seduction.

This is the only object in secretion and speech.

Dance a clean dream and an extravagant turn up… show the choice and make no more mistakes than yesterday.

Boycunt. Writing. Love. Make no more mistakes than the day can hold the day can hold all of this juiced.

Re/produced.

ACKNOWLEDGEMENTS

Many of the poems in this book have been read aloud, most often from the stage of Hares & Hyenas Bookshop in Fitzroy, Melbourne. Thank you Crusader and Rowland for having faith in my writing and work, and for giving me stage space to perform this work.

Thank you to Pam Brown, Kevin Brophy, Jean Kent, Susan Bradley-Smith, Jessica Wilkinson, Paul Hetherington, Shane Strange, Jen Webb, Donna Lee Brien, Anna Poletti, Julia Prendergast, and many other poets and writers along the way, who told me to keep sending this book into the world (especially when it felt too hard to do so).

I am indebted to Marion May Campbell for her mentorship, her many kindnesses, and for the words 'small children do not splash or cry out' which come from her book *Fragments from a Paper Witch*.

Thank you to La Trobe University and The English, Theatre and Drama Disciplinary Research Program, who continue to support my writing through small grants, which always seem to come just at the right time.

Finally, thank you to Terri-ann White and UWAP for taking *Rallying*, and for turning it into such a beautiful book.

Some of the poems and prose pieces in this work have appeared in the following places:

Eades, Q. (2016) Tender Bodies: Boycunt, Writing, Love, in *Runway: Australian Experimental Art*, Issue 32: Re/production.

Eades, Q. (2016) Coalesce, in *Cordite: The End* (53.0).

Eades, Q. (2015) various, in all the beginnings: a queer autobiography of the body, Tantanoola, North Melbourne.

Quinn, K. (2015) 'How to disappear in your name', in *TEXT Journal*, Special Issue 30: Creative Writing as Research IV. Eds Krauth, Brien, Watkins, Baker, Lawrence, & Costello.

Quinn, K. (2015) Black Saturday Findings, in *Rabbit: A Journal For Non Fiction Poetry*, Issue 15.

Quinn, K. (2015) In the Alfama, and On the Metro, in *Axon: Creative Explorations* (Vol 5, No 1).

Quinn, K. (2014) Salt remembers, in *Feral Feminisms* (Issue 2, Summer).

Quinn, K. (2014) Coming and Going, in *Grieve, 2014*. Newcastle: Hunter Writers Centre.

Quinn, K. (2014) Ash and Breath, in *A Slow Combusting Hymn: poetry from and about Newcastle and the Hunter Region*. ASM and Cerebrus Press, Macao & Buladelah.

Quinn, K. (2014) Rallying, in *Cordite* (46.0).

Quinn, K. (2013) Always going home (a domestic cycle), in *Now you shall know: Newcastle poetry prize anthology 2013*. Newcastle: Hunter Writers Centre.

Quinn, K. (2011) The second cup. In S. Stanford (Ed.), *An attitude of cups*. Melbourne: Melbourne Poets Union.

www.ingramcontent.com/pod-product-compliance
Lightning Source LLC
Chambersburg PA
CBHW020333170426
43200CB00006B/369